Coaching Emotional Intelligence in the Classroom

Coaching Emotional Intelligence in the Classroom is a practical resource to help Key Stage 2 and Key Stage 3 teachers explore and understand a range of concepts, principles and techniques gathered under the term 'emotional intelligence', and the way that this powerfully influences pupils' behaviour and learning in the classroom. Creative activities are suggested throughout, leading towards a more explicit focus on coaching methods to help pupils become independent, creative and effective learners able to set goals, generate ideas, solve problems and arrive at reasoned decisions.

This book focuses on five key areas:

- self-awareness;
- innovative and inventive thinking;
- independent enquiry;
- collaborative learning;
- communication skills.

Dealing in an engaging way with social and emotional aspects of learning, personalised learning, thinking skills and social inclusion, the authors offer teachers all of the necessary tools to help pupils build life- and people-skills which will extend beyond school. It will be of interest to all practising teachers, teaching assistants and school counsellors working with young people.

Steve Bowkett is a full-time writer, storyteller, educational consultant and hypnotherapist. He is the author of more than fifty books, including the *Countdown* series of books for Routledge.

Simon Percival is a former teacher who as a qualified and experienced coach now runs his own practice helping individuals, including students, reach their personal and professional goals.

The authors offer PeopleWise workshop sessions for pupils, and INSET that extend the techniques in the book to demonstrate what creative coaching in the classroom looks like, sounds like, feels like.

Coaching Emotional Intelligence in the Classroom

A practical guide for 7-14

Steve Bowkett and Simon Percival

 Routledge
Taylor & Francis Group

LONDON AND NEW YORK

This first edition published 2011
by Routledge
2 Park Square, Milton Park, Abingdon, Oxon, OX14 4RN

Simultaneously published in the USA and Canada
by Routledge
270 Madison Avenue, New York, NY 10016

Routledge is an imprint of the Taylor & Francis Group, an informa business

© 2011 Steve Bowkett and Simon Percival

Typeset in Bembo by Glyph International

Printed and bound in Great Britain by
CPI Antony Rowe, Chippenham, Wiltshire

British Library Cataloguing in Publication Data
A catalogue record for this book is available from the British Library

Library of Congress Cataloging-in-Publication Data
Bowkett, Stephen.
Coaching emotional intelligence in the classroom : a practical guide for
7-14 / By Steve Bowkett and Simon Percival. – 3rd ed.
p. cm.
Includes index.
1. Affective education–Handbooks, manuals, etc. 2. Emotional
intelligence–Study and teaching. I. Percival, Simon. II. Title.
LB1072.B69 2011
370.15'34–dc22   2010028617

ISBN13: 978-0-415-57779-3 (hbk)
ISBN13: 978-0-415-57780-9 (pbk)
ISBN13: 978-0-203-83337-7 (ebk)

Contents

List of Illustrations

Introduction

Welcome to *Coaching Emotional Intelligence in the Classroom*, a practical handbook that will help you nurture the emotional intelligence (EI) of those you teach whilst developing their coaching skills. The activities in this book seek to uncover and highlight for the children those aspects that make up EI in much the same way as a coach will ask questions to uncover and highlight an individual's resourcefulness. We don't believe that you can tell someone how to be emotionally intelligent in the same way that knowing the skills of coaching will not make you a coach; discovery, awareness, questioning, consideration, acceptance, practice and application will move the individual forward. That is what we have set out to encourage.

The need to become peoplewise

In 2007 UNICEF published a report that caused ripples throughout much of the developed world. 'An Overview of Child Well-Being in Rich Countries' provided a comprehensive assessment of the context in which children were being brought up in 21 of the most economically advanced countries. When the rankings for six dimensions of well-being were averaged, the UK was placed bottom overall. Its best ranking was twelfth for Health and Safety (infant death, accidents, immunizations) and the worst were for family and peer relationships, behaviours and risks, and subjective well-being (bottom of each dimension). One place above the UK was the US, economically the richest nation in the world. France also languished in the bottom third of countries and Germany only made it to mid-table. The reports' authors found 'no obvious relationship' between children's well-being and how rich the country was in which they lived. However, regardless of wealth, should not all children be entitled to an upbringing which is safe, healthy and loving, and filled with compassion, quality relationships and opportunity?

A way forward for peoplewisdom

Knowing how what we do affects others and a better grasp of so-called 'soft skills' would be a good start. Understanding how to identify goals, generate ideas, make independent judgements, reach reasoned decisions and formulate a plan would also go some way to us seeing how we can help ourselves. These are only some of the aspects of *Coaching Emotional Intelligence in the Classroom*.

This book is underpinned by a creative/thinking skills agenda, at the heart of which is the 'creative attitude' which includes the key elements of noticing and questioning. We encourage children to think – about themselves, their thoughts, their actions, about others – and act in an emotionally intelligent manner whilst striving for their goals. We also highlight the importance of the children's creativity in the coaching we advocate.

In the earlier sections we introduce activities to develop the EI of the children, which also provide some of the foundations for the 'creative coaching'. In the later sections we build upon this to explicitly develop coaching, which can be utilised with the children to develop EI in themselves and in others. It also supports current initiatives in the UK education system. Namely, it:

1. Links to Every Child Matters:
    a. Be healthy – making the right lifestyle decisions for themselves; promoting mental well-being through better relationships with others and help with alleviating stress in challenging situations, for example.
    b. Enjoy and achieve – improving thinking skills and the creative attitude that can be transferred between school, work and social situations; developing resilience and resourcefulness.
    c. Make a positive contribution – developing 'well-rounded' citizens, who contribute to their communities and enhance the lives of the people they meet.
    d. Stay safe – becoming more judicious in what they do and the choices they make; improving confidence to communicate their choices.
    e. Achieve economic well-being – developing those important 'soft skills' alongside content knowledge.
2. Explicitly promotes five of the six areas of the Personal Learning and Thinking Skills (PLTS) framework – inquisitiveness, collaboration, self-management, reflection and creativity.
3. Supports the SEAL curriculum.
4. Addresses all three of the broad curriculum aims for the primary and secondary curricula (successful learners, confident individuals and responsible citizens).
5. Deals directly with three of the six 'essentials for learning and life' in the primary curriculum (personal and emotional skills, social skills, learning and thinking skills) and can have a positive impact on the other three (literacy, numeracy and ICT).

We hope that you will use this book as more than a classroom resource to work through; we imagine it being used flexibly and dynamically to excite the best from your learners according to their needs. Ultimately, we hope for its suggestions to be not only practised, but applied, modelled and reinforced. Used wisely, wonderful things could happen.

1

El basic skills

We would like to suggest that a sound basis for developing emotional intelligence to any useful degree includes the key elements of –

- Awareness of self
- Awareness of others.

The creative coaching activities that follow will help develop these two ideas. Both elements evolve out of our natural curiosity, the ability (and the tendency) we have to 'be nosy', in other words to notice and to question. The suggestions in this book will help refine our exploratory nature, which informs the aims and the structure of this book.

We can begin to map out these broad notions under the headings of –

- Reflective Thinking. This includes engaging with philosophical ideas and moral dilemmas, asking questions that explore values, considering options, forming judgements, reaching conclusions and making decisions.
- Metacognition. This means noticing and thinking about the thinking we do. It presupposes the evolving ability to internalise the attention and to become increasingly aware of the connections between our thoughts and feelings (and the reactions that may follow from them).
- Empathy. Being able to appreciate how the world looks from another's perspective. Although ultimately this is an act of the imagination (since we can never truly know another's reality), it has validity since we are all linked by a network of human experiences and reactions.
- Creativity. This makes active use of two basic human resources, those of memory and imagination. Memory in this sense is not just our ability to consciously recall or remember particular incidents. Our 'map of memory' (misleadingly but frequently called the 'map of reality') operates largely at a subconscious level. What we have previously experienced allows us to make sense of the world now, as we function within it moment by moment.[1]

Imagination is the incredible power we possess to form mental constructions (thoughts, ideas, scenarios) that need to have nothing to do with our immediate experience. The creative use of imagination necessitates making new connections – i.e. moving away from so-called 'routine thinking' – by exploring things in as many different ways as we can.

The effort to forge new links, making a larger and more elaborate idea from two or more simpler ones, keeps our thinking fresh, flexible and dynamic. Furthermore, changing a perspective can also generate new insights that allow us to make progress in our lives (Notice that 'routine' rendered down becomes 'rut'.)

As a way of dipping our toe in the water of these ideas, here are some quick and simple activities that you can try out with your group.

1. What-If Scenarios. These can be quickly and easily created and focussed on any topic area. Once a what-if question has been asked, append these three sub-questions–
    ■ What would the world be like?
    ■ What problems might we face?
    ■ How can we try to solve those problems?

Some of the what-ifs we've used in the past, and which might be more immediately pertinent to the themes of this book include:

a. What if people changed colour depending on the feelings they were having? (So as well as blushing red with embarrassment or turning white with fear, we actually would go green with envy, yellow through cowardice etc.)
b. What if your thoughts could be read by anyone for five minutes every day? (You don't know when that five minutes will happen and you don't know who might be looking in on your mind. Scary!)
c. What if every five years everyone had to change places with someone else in the world? And it could be anyone! (Decide whether this means just doing their job, living with their family etc., or actually inhabiting their body.)
d. What if global warming happened much more quickly than everyone has predicted, and that within twenty years half of the presently habitable land in the world becomes a desert?
e. What if people became physically bigger depending on how intelligent they were? (This opens up the can of worms of what 'intelligence' means. It also leads quickly into philosophical discussions and political debates… Maybe not such a quick and simple activity as we promised!) Other ideas the children might enjoy are:
    ■ What if nobody ever figured out how to do Maths?
    ■ What if an asteroid had not made the dinosaurs extinct?
    ■ What if George Bush had not given up drinking? (okay, too political)

Note: If you run a what-if game, be prepared to think on your feet as children ask questions about the basic premise. The only rule is that once an answer is given, everyone has to stick by that decision.

2. Mini Moral Dilemmas. These are situations, briefly described, that prompt children to reflect on how they might feel and react. Once your group becomes familiar with the idea, children can make them up for themselves. So for example…
    a. You find a wallet in the street. It contains £100 and nothing else. What would you do? Would your reaction be different if you found the wallet in the middle

of the countryside, with no houses for miles? What if the wallet also contained the business card of a local window cleaner? What if it contained the card of a local and very successful businessman? Would any of your reactions be different if the wallet contained £1,000?

b. You discover that your best friend has somehow got hold of the answers to an important test that you must both take the next day. In other words, your friend intends to cheat. What do you do? What if you thought you were likely to fail the test unless your friend shared the answers with you? Would your reaction be different if you were confident of passing the test through your own abilities?

c. You discover that you have a rare blood type. By an incredible coincidence, your favourite celebrity has the same blood type and becomes ill – but can be saved by a blood transfusion. Would you offer to donate blood? What if your gift shortened your life by five years? Would you still donate blood if the person who needed it was someone you didn't like?

Note: An excellent little book filled with similar dilemmas is Gregory Stock's *The Book of Questions* (see Bibliography). It's intended for an adult readership, but many of the questions and scenarios can be adapted for children to consider.

3. Simile Game. Make up similes (or metaphors) for a range of feelings. Encourage the children to be as playful and off-the-wall as they like…
    ■ As angry as a bee on a dead flower.
    ■ As frustrated as a caged rabbit looking out over a field.
    ■ As excited as a firework about to explode.
    ■ As relaxed as a cat on a sunny doorstep.
    ■ Envy is a grey coat beside a bright party dress.
    ■ Joy is a snowman listening to a forecast for more snow.
    ■ Fear is walking down a lonely midnight street forever.
    ■ Friendship is when neither of you will take that last chocolate for yourself.

4. Simple Linking. Assemble a dozen or so objects or pictures and prompt children to forge links by saying, 'Choose two of these and if you were going to use them in a story, what would your story be about?' Also ask for the story to be summarised in just a sentence or two. So looking at the selection in Fig. 1.1 below…

5. Empathy Circles. This activity encourages children to 'put themselves in someone else's shoes' to consider how they feel. Draw a large circle to represent an angry person, a jealous person, or whatever the focus is going to be. Prepare a number of other, smaller circles (though of varying sizes) to represent thoughts, feelings and insights. Working in groups, ask children to put on the smaller circles, words and pictures representing the thoughts and feelings going on inside that person. The different sizes of the circles stand for the degree of significance of that thought or feeling in the person's life. When a circle has been prepared, ask the group to position it carefully in the main circle. Explain that putting it entirely within the main circle means that the thought or feeling is being kept hidden. If the smaller circle overlaps the larger one, the thought or feeling is being expressed in some way. See Figure 1.2.

Figure 1.1 Linking game

6. Stepping in and out of the Picture. Find a suitable picture and tell the children that you will count to three. On the count of three they must use their imagination to 'step into' the picture, where they'll be able to notice colours, sounds, textures, objects, people 'beyond the frame' and lots of other interesting details. Collect their impressions, then count 'three–two–one, now step back out of the picture'.

Use the same picture on another occasion. This time explain that when the children step into the picture, they will be, for example, a person going for an important job interview, or an older person living alone, or someone who's just had a quarrel with their partner. Say 'And what thoughts and feelings do you notice now?' Repeat this activity several times over a number of weeks, giving children the experience of mentally changing their perspective.

Figure 1.2 Empathy circles

In the picture below, before the children step in each time, create a different relationship between the two people being portrayed –

- A wife coming home from work finding her husband having an angry phone conversation.
- The man's daughter dropping by unexpectedly after being away for some months.
- The woman walking out on the man because she's tired of his moodiness.
- Invite the class to come up with other ideas.

Tips

- You can combine this activity with the Empathy Circles game above.
- It's worth pointing out that actually *no one knows* what's going on between the two people, but how easy it is to speculate and put our own interpretation on things!

7. Similar Feelings. This is a discussion activity where you encourage children to explore the differences between apparently similar feelings. So, for instance, what differences

Figure 1.3 Through the window

exist between resentment and jealousy? How about differences between being angry and being furious? Or between joy and happiness?

It's not necessary for children to remember occasions when they experienced the feelings in question. The aim is simply to compare ideas and viewpoints.

Tip: Look in a thesaurus for literally hundreds of words, handily categorised, spanning the emotional spectrum.

One way of approaching the activity is to imagine the feeling as an object or shape that you can hold. If we were dealing with happiness for instance, ask a child 'If you could hold that feeling in your hands, what shape would it have?[2] And what's its colour? Size? Texture? Weight? Temperature?' Go through all the senses until the child has a clear representation of the feeling in mind. Now say 'The feeling is turning into excitement. Notice how it changes – tell me as you notice'.

8.   World Wide Web. This encourages children to connect their own lives with others' and to appreciate 'the bigger picture'. Here are a couple of variations…
     ■   Ask children to look in their grocery cupboard and make a list of its contents and where they come from (not 'the supermarket', but countries of origin). The activity becomes even richer and more interesting if children actually go to the supermarket and look at a wider range of goods.

Tip: In one school Steve visited the children used a large world map and connected where they were in the UK to all the places their sampled range of foodstuffs came from. The result actually looked like a web!

■ Create a chain of thought linking a simple, everyday activity to its wider context. The example we offer children is making a cup of tea...

I put the tea in the cup. Who put the tea in the teabag? – Who packed the teabags in their box? – Who put the box on the shelf in the shop? – Who delivered the box to the store? – Who loaded the box on the truck at the warehouse? – Who delivered the box to the warehouse? Who processed the tea to put in the teabags to put in the box? Who brought the leaves from where they were grown? Who brought the leaves from the plantations to the packing plant? Who picked the leaves that ended up in my cup?

(One child who created a chain something like this wrote 'Thank you, whoever you are' at the end.)

2

Coaching, creativity and EI: the connection

We have already suggested that creativity is an important aspect of developing both emotional intelligence and the application of 'coaching'. While this has been defined in various ways, we feel that useful components of coaching include those laid out below in Table 2.1.

In saying this we emphasise that coaching is not seen as a form of therapy. No 'dysfunction' of the coachee is implied. Also, coaching in a strict sense is future oriented, using a person's ability to make decisions in the present moment as the driving force towards moving in a desired direction. Throughout this book, coaching skills and techniques are practised as part of the broader aim of becoming more emotionally intelligent. Without entering into a lengthy discussion of the subject, emotional intelligence can be defined as the potential we have for understanding what influences our thoughts, feelings and subsequent responses and how we can manipulate this information for our own well-being and harmonious relationships with others. This is of course a vague thing to say, although we can begin to focus in on more precise ideas by bearing the following in mind –

- Intelligence is not directly correlated in this case with IQ (however *that* may be defined) or academic ability. (For instance 'John', a friend of Steve's has been assessed as a mathematical genius, but whose incredible abilities have for years been blocked by emotional difficulties. John has attempted a Ph.D. on several occasions, only to drop out of the course for medical reasons linked to that vague and all-encompassing notion of 'stress' and bouts of deep depression. While this may be an extreme example, John lies along a continuum familiar to many people, both adults and children.) An important implication of this idea for us is that all children, whatever their academic ability, can become more emotionally intelligent.
- If our idea of intelligence involves the 'manipulation' of information, then we define manipulation as 'skillful handling', from the Latin *manus*, 'hand'. 'Information' itself might be seen as 'in-formation', the active construction of new meanings and understandings out of our experiences. This in turn means that we are not talking about the passive acceptance of knowledge (including advice or guidance) within the coaching context.

All of this leads to the conclusion that such handling of information is direct, personal and unique to the individual 'handler', which in turn presupposes that anyone coaching

Table 2.1 Useful components of coaching include

Maximising potential in a chosen direction...	...whilst being aware of thoughts and feelings (which encompass, fears, desires, limiting and liberating beliefs, and values)...	...leading to strategies for exploring judgements, reaching conclusions, making decisions...	...and so helping oneself (and others) to achieve personal goals and, ultimately, confident autonomy and solution-focused thinking.
Samuel Johnson once said that, 'It is a most mortifying reflection for a man to consider what he has done, compared to what he might have done'. Coaching seeks to help individuals avoid such regret and move them towards their goals. Coachees choose their own goals in line with what they ultimately want to achieve. The coach helps crystallise these into specific, stepped plans where progress can be seen and celebrated.	Emotionally intelligent people will have a sound awareness of themselves, yet may still have fears and beliefs that hinder progress. There is always a choice in how we respond to such things. Coaching is a process that can help coachees recognise these choices and overcome potential limitations, just as it can help ourselves and others move towards developing an emotionally intelligent disposition. An effective coach will challenge coaehees to address obstacles, and support them in their progress by providing feedback and questions to prompt resourceful thinking.	Esteemed by the success of clearing away any obstacles and with (re)affirmed belief in their own resourcefulness, coachees will feel ready to explore further progress towards goals. A coach will listen attentively and question pertinently to help open up the coaehee's thinking, prompt his/her creativity, find a way forward that is best for his/her and then formulate a plan of action. With a little practice we can learn how to self-coach and do all of the above for ourselves.	The short-term and medium-term goals of coaching are to get the coachee to where s/he wants to be. However, the unstated goal of each coaching session is to build self-reliance and empower him/her to take control of their lives. Repeated exposure to the process, to the tacit belief that coaches have in an individual's resourcefulness, and to their own successes can gradually instill the confidence and provide the tools with which coachees can address goals and challenges with resolute self-belief

others does not make suggestions, offer advice or in any way assume the mantle of the 'guru'. A coach creates opportunities for people to realise their potential. Someone *self-coaching* – perhaps a more difficult process – must find the wherewithal to look at their own situation from an altered perspective coupled with the ability to bring flexible thinking and fresh insights to that situation…

Which brings us back to the creative connection.

In our work in schools we talk with children about 'the creative attitude'. This arises from the natural curiosity we all possess and often takes the form of noticing and asking questions – more on this in the next unit. We feel also that a creatively active person will show some or all of the following attributes –

- A good sense of humour.
- Playfulness that takes many forms.
- Tolerance of others' ideas.
- A healthy resilience to setbacks (which are usually seen as further opportunities for learning).
- Independence of judgement when ideas and issues have been explored.
- A growing realisation that the mind is amazing and can think in many ways; different kinds of thinking being seen as a well-stocked box of instruments, coupled with insightfulness in deciding which instrument(s) to pick for the job in hand.
- Feeling comfortable in the presence of uncertainty and ambiguity (perhaps bearing in mind Einstein's aphorism that out of chaos, order often emerges).
- An increasing degree of self-esteem. For us this most truly means 'self-estimation', built on positive thoughts, feelings and actions. Again this is a proactive force that leads towards honesty and transparency in making judgements about how we estimate ourselves. The acceptance and approval of others can feel good, but is not the major component in building *self*-esteem.

Activities

1. The 'Playfulness Is…' Game. You may know of the *Love Is…* comic illustrations which were created by Kim Caseli in the 1960s and that have appeared widely in newspapers and magazines ever since. The idea can be adapted to help children think about the qualities that make up the creative attitude. So for instance you can play the 'Playfulness Is…' (or 'Playfulness Means…') game.

Write 'playfulness is / means' on a large sheet of paper or in the centre of what will become a wall display. Invite the children to offer their ideas in the form of words and pictures. Give them a few examples to establish the point of the task.

- Playfulness means thinking of a hundred things you can use a paperclip for.
- Playfulness is trying things out in a different way.
- Playfulness is doing a silly walk just for the fun of it.

- Playfulness means understanding someone else's point of view.
- Playfulness is imagining six impossible things before breakfast (after Lewis Carroll).

Note: Your kickstart-examples will obviously vary depending on the age of the children involved. A few of the above are more sophisticated ideas. This is not to say that younger children won't cope with them. In fact, you might note children's puzzled expressions and decide this is a great opportunity to explore ideas further (thus helping the children to feel more comfortable in the presence of uncertainty).

You can develop the activity by using some of the children's responses as a basis for further discussion. In our 'A Good Sense of Humour Means…' workshop we threw in the idea that 'A good sense of humour means laughing at everyone's jokes even if they aren't funny'. Some children immediately questioned or disagreed with this (which is what we wanted to happen) and we then discussed subtopics such as –

- How do we know something is a joke?
- Why do we laugh (we collected lots of reasons)?
- When is it impolite / offensive / wrong to laugh? Why?

We also set up a Laughometer to rate the funniness of jokes. We lined up six jokes for children to rank on a 1 to 5 scale of funniness. Then we totaled up the scores. The winner on this occasion was… What was King Arthur's favourite game? Knights and crosses (made us laugh too).

2.   The Points-of-View Game. This activity helps children to appreciate different and opposing points of view.

Prepare for the game by raising an issue that will generate a range of opinions. Ask children to decide where they stand in the matter, then group them so that all the children in any given group have similar views. Ask the groups to discuss the topic from their point of view for a short time.

When they have 'rehearsed' their arguments, ask each group to think of *counter* arguments to their ideas. Each group has now experienced two different ways of looking at things.

The activity can culminate in various ways:

- Arrange a whole class debate where children have to discuss the topic from a viewpoint that is different from or opposite to their own. You may want to nominate at least one group as 'neutral observers', whose job is to assess the validity or robustness of the other groups' ideas.
- Have each group make a list of points for and against on separate scraps of paper. Then arrange the scraps in terms of facts versus opinions and / or relevance to the argument, where the most compelling point is placed at the top of the list.

Note: For more information on developing arguments and discussions of this kind see Steve's *Countdown to Non-Fiction Writing*.

3. Wordplay Games. We touched on wordplay in the previous unit (the Simile Game on page 5). Such games can take many forms, but most or all of them implicitly reinforce the ideas that while words influence thoughts and thus perceptions, language is flexible and can be moulded. Actively engaging with language and forging it into new shapes to see what effects that has also begins to prepare the ground for recognising and changing the metaphors we use to build our 'frameworks of reality'. This in itself is a large and rapidly growing field of enquiry that we will look at in more detail later. But for now…

- Phrase Flips. These are like very brief Spoonerisms, where phonemes or syllables are switched between words for comic effect. A well-known Spoonerism is 'Go for a ride on a well-boiled icicle' as opposed to the 'routine' arrangement of 'Go for a ride on a well-oiled bicycle'. Some phrase flips we like are – a math bat / as mean as custard / cross the road when you see the mean gran / would you like some keys and parrots with your pie? Ask children to notice the image that comes to mind as they create a meaningful phrase flip, thus giving them practise in metacognition (see page 3).

Note: Many phrase flips won't make sense. For every ten experiments children might hit upon one that works. However, even this phenomenon illustrates the important creative principle that *to have good ideas you need to have lots of ideas*. More implicitly the game demonstrates Thomas Edison's conviction that (in this case) a phrase flip that doesn't work isn't a failure; it's another step along the road to success (and in line with the notion that practice doesn't make perfect, but makes *better*).

- Proverb Twists. Building on phrase flips, 'tweak' proverbs into new meanings…
  - A rose by any other name would smell as sweat.
  - A mule and his honey are soon parted.
  - In for a Lenny, in for a round.
  - Putting the heart before the course.
  - Stocks and phones will break no tones.
  - Don't put all your legs in one casket.

- Tom Swifties. These are varieties of pun. The simplest make use of ly-adverbs.
  - 'Ouch! I've cut myself with these scissors', Tom said sharply.
  - 'Fido, stop chasing my cat!' Tom insisted doggedly.
  - 'You're coming to jail, my lad', said Inspector Tom arrestingly.
  - 'Where have you put my pencil sharpener'? Tom asked bluntly.
  - 'It's OK, I've found it now', Tom added pointedly.
  - 'I'm boldly going where no one has gone before', Tom said enterprisingly.

Slightly more sophisticated Tom Swifties link the description of Tom's reply with what he actually says.

- 'The woodwind section of this orchestra is excellent', Tom piped up.
- 'I'm sorry the pudding is so awful', said Tom, his confidence crumbling.

- 'I've lost my football', Tom sounded so disappointed – though bounced back moments later when he found it.
- (And Steve's own favourite) ' I think I've got a split personality', Tom said being frank.

Note: You'll find more on wordplay in *Jumpstart! Creativity* (see Bibliography).

3

Encouraging creativity

We hope you find that the games and activities we've already looked at help to encourage creativity. If we take as our – simplistic but useful – working definition that creativity involves making new connections and taking multiple perspectives, then any activity that satisfies either or both of these criteria is *per se* a creative one.

We've also suggested that creativity frequently shows itself through noticing things and through asking questions. These are specific observable behaviours from the children which as adults we can notice, verify and approve of. So when we're playing the phrase flip game and Sarah says 'A bat casket!' our reply of 'Well done Sarah that's a clever flip' applies those two powerful motivators for her and other children to keep trying –

- Quick feedback
- Sincere praise.

Even such simple interactions as this encourage creativity. And it's worth noting our belief that to en-courage means 'to give courage to'. Children may not feel comfortable and confident enough in themselves to try out the tasks we ask them to do. Even early on in their educational careers children can be frightened of the wrong answer, of looking foolish, of being negatively judged or compared with others. So it's incumbent upon us not only to model the attitude we're looking for (yes, we've got to be playful too) but to actively create 'positive feedback loops' that allow children to realise we value their thinking. This is of fundamental importance – the idea that we 'value it before we have to evaluate'.

There are many, many ways of practising noticing and questioning in the classroom through the ethos of playful exploration. Major benefits of running what might otherwise seem like trivial or inconsequential games are that children –

- Are soon likely to transfer the skills to other subject areas in the curriculum.
- With practice will become increasingly sophisticated and effective 'noticers and questioners'.
- Are developing life skills that will be of benefit beyond school.
- Will soon be able to create further resources for themselves – most immediately for more sophisticated versions of the games themselves, but later across a broader field. Any such contribution helps to underpin the notion that 'we are resourceful', a vital insight in coaching EI.

Whilst co-writing *Thinking for Learning* Simon was told time and again by children in lessons he was observing that thinking skills sessions were fun because of the 'playful' element to many. Later in the lessons (and no doubt in the children's school careers) the quality of learning revealed the useful thinking and transfer of skills that was taking place.

Activities

1. Spot the difference. Using a picture pair, such as the example below, ask the children to spot as many differences as they can. Solution is on page 116.

    Tip: Children can make their own versions of this activity as they practise their ICT skills by using even simple graphics packages.

2. Observation Tray. Put ten or so small objects in a tray, change one each day and ask the children to notice the swap. You can increase the challenge of the game by putting more objects in the tray and swapping two or more each day.
3. Change one thing in your classroom every few days, perhaps by removing or replacing part of a display; ask the children to recall the information that was there.
4. Text Tweak. This is like spot the difference using words. Make a few small changes to a paragraph or page of text. Invite the children not only to notice what has

Figure 3.1 Spot the difference

changed but also how the alterations affect the meaning and how the sentences would sound if read aloud. Used with poems, this is a good way into discussing its features and effects.

5.   Body Posture. Ask volunteers to assume postures that suggest certain emotions and / or scenarios. Other children as observers say what they think is going on.

Take it further: A powerful question in coaching is 'What would have to change for X to become Y?' You can introduce the idea in this activity. Suppose Tonita assumed a body posture and facial expression indicating anger. Ask the class what would have to change for Tonita to appear happy. Draw out as much information from the class as you can, even down to the positioning of the subject's eyebrows! This 'drawing out' focuses attention on smaller details (so sharpening observational skills) and begins to split the overall impression of anger into smaller and more specific 'chunks'. It also raises awareness of *what a person is doing to achieve that state* of anger or happiness etc.). Thus the children come to see the relationship between awareness, understanding and control – in this case of their emotional responses...

■   This is what I'm doing[1] to be angry.
■   I'm making connections between what's going on around me and my own thoughts and feelings.
■   By doing such-and-such I can change X to Y.[2]

6.   A Cloud of Questions. This simple game raises the profile of questioning behaviour in the classroom. The idea is to show the class a picture or object and ask the children to ask questions about it. That's all. The aim is to assemble as many questions as possible within the time frame – and also questions about the questions, as appropriate. This generates a mass of 'raw material' that you can then reflect upon...
    ■   Which questions do we know the answers to?
    ■   Which questions have more than one answer?
    ■   Which questions do we think can't be answered (and why)?
    ■   Are there certain questions that need to be answered before others can be tackled?
    ■   Are some questions more important (or relevant or significant [is there a difference?]) than others? How can we decide?

Running this process in turn leads to the powerful 'Three-Step Method' of making progress –

■   What do we know? (And how do we know we know?)
■   What do we think we know?
■   What can we ask or do to find out more?

This strategy can be applied in any subject area and helps to 'tease out' verifiable knowledge from inferences, assumptions, speculations, generalisations and other aspects of our thinking. Fundamentally it helps to *make thinking more explicit*, a necessary precursor to developing both thinking skills and EI (if indeed there is any difference).

In running the activity several times children will come to see that some questions have one right answer, others have many (right?) answers, while yet others seem not to be answerable in any definitive or final way.

7. This leads us into the field of philosophical enquiry, which seems to be growing in popularity in schools. There is no scope in this book to explore P4C (philosophy for children) other than to introduce and recommend it. You'll find some references in the Bibliography. But in approaching P4C we mention to children that –

    - Some questions seem not to have any right answer, or at least one that everybody can agree upon.
    - It's okay not to know the answer in these cases.
    - Often questions like these, as we try to answer them, lead us into more questions! That's what makes such questions so very interesting...
        - What exactly is it that makes me who I am?
        - What's the difference between a live rat and a dead rat?
        - Is the past real?
        - Is the future set (as Sarah Connor might say)?
        - Why does the universe exist at all? This is regarded as one of the most fundamental philosophical questions – why is there something rather than nothing? Putting that into Google by the way pulls up 21 million references!

Happy questioning.

4

Conscious and subconscious

Although we've already made the point that coaching emphasises conscious reasoning and what might be called logical intelligence, our thoughts and feelings are also the ongoing outcomes of much subconscious activity (or 'processing') that happens as it were behind the scenes, largely outside the realm of our conscious awareness. So for instance, to take a negative example, let's say that Jane feels anxious but doesn't really know why. Everything seems to be fine in her life and there are no obvious or logical reasons to worry. And yet the feeling won't subside – in fact dwelling on it can even make it worse. In this case the insights mentioned in the previous section appear to be of little use –

- This is what I'm doing to be anxious.
- I'm making connections between what's going on around me and my own thoughts and feelings.
- By doing such-and-such I can change anxiety to reassurance.

Jane really may not know what she's 'doing' to generate the anxiety and indeed might say that she isn't doing anything at all; she just feels anxious. There seem to be no connections between the feelings and her current life circumstances, in which case strategies for change appear to be thin on the ground.

Various therapies (for example hypnotherapy and other kinds of psychotherapy) work with the subconscious and either endeavour to uncover the root cause of the problem, or at least attempt to utilise the subconscious resource directly to resolve the issue. Coaching however, which is not a therapy, works cognitively. So what steps can be taken to deal with the feeling?

As a start Jane can acknowledge that 'the subconscious is at work'. People are usually not purposeless and feelings frequently happen for reasons – in Jane's case reasons that are subconscious; that either have been forgotten or that were never consciously recognised in the first place. Several insights can begin to address this situation –

1. The subconscious is part of my whole self. It is doing its best for me and is not 'out to get me'. (Some people feel as though they constantly sabotage themselves in different ways: although there may be a subconscious agenda of self-punishment, this is quite uncommon and may in any case be addressed by cognitive techniques.)

2. The subconscious is like the automatic pilot of my personality. It often works for reasons, based on instructions that it received. But those instructions are not helpful to me now. The reasons (in this case for the anxiety) whatever they might be are a hindrance.

3. What I consciously think about I subconsciously react to. So if I'm thinking about being anxious, my automatic pilot reacts with feelings of anxiety. This is also true if I try *not* to feel anxious. Thinking 'I must not worry' still brings the idea of worry to mind, and therefore I react to it. This means that by changing my conscious thoughts I can begin to modify the subconscious reaction and 'turn down' the anxiety.

So what can Jane do to modify the subconsciously generated anxiety response? There are literally scores of techniques. Here are some that, we've found, are easy to use and have been effective on many occasions…

■   DPA – Direct Positive Action. This is more of a general principle, which says that doing something is always better than doing nothing. Doing nothing usually means simply dwelling on one's present state or, as the saying goes, wallowing in one's misery. Once Jane has decided to take action, *that very intention* can begin to have a positive influence on the negative subconscious response. DPAs can include the following –

   ■   Metacognition. Noticing one's own thoughts and the feelings that arise from them. Part of the 'automatic pilot syndrome' is that habitual thoughts can circulate through the conscious mind without really being noticed or acted upon. It's easy to lose oneself in thought, to drift rather aimlessly from image to image, from memory to memory. If such memories are negative, then the end result is that we have evoked these unpleasant experiences unwittingly, feel low as a consequence yet have done nothing about it. One easy way of demonstrating metacognition to the children is to read them a descriptive paragraph from a story and then ask the children what they imagined – what images, sounds and other impressions went through their minds.

   ■   Change the script. As soon as we begin to catch ourselves in such unhelpful idle daydreaming, we can change the way we think. Steve recalls an argument he was once involved in and previously felt upset and angry each time it came to mind. Then he decided that it was *his* memory and he could do what he wanted with it. So he thought of it again and this time caused his 'opponent' to drop into a very deep hole in the ground. He imagined this scenario in as much detail as possible and played it through in his head repeatedly. The result was that if the experience now 'pops into his mind' automatically it's the modified memory Steve recalls, not the original one (you'd need to make an effort of will to get that one). A further benefit is that the anger and upset attached to the original experience has now transformed into amusement – or malicious glee, depending on Steve's mood. Help children to do this by asking them to recall their impressions of the descriptive paragraph you read, then encourage them to deliberately change colours, sounds, etc. in various ways.

■ Artworks. Or art works. Unpleasant feelings can be represented either in the imagination or on paper as pieces of abstract art. If on paper, invite children to paint the anxiety (or whatever feeling they want to work with), allowing themselves to 'go with the flow' rather than trying to consciously think of which brushstrokes to make. Simply let them become passive observers of the creative act. Once the work seems to be finished, tell children to redraw / repaint the picture deliberately choosing different colours, shapes and configurations. Then consign the original to the recycle bin. If the technique is done mentally, instruct the class to imagine the feeling as powerfully as possible using all of the senses. Ask children to decide where it has been lodging in the body. Then redesign it sense by sense, detail by detail. When everything has changed, push it somewhere else inside oneself and notice how it feels now.

■ Letter to Self. Explain to children that if they suspect or know that unpleasant feelings have resulted from things that happened when they were younger, write a letter to that younger self pointing out –

    ■ That the older you-of-now understands and is always there to help and support and guide.

    ■ That the younger you will not be blamed or judged.

    ■ That younger you has made an invaluable contribution to the more grown-up person you are now.

    ■ That you need younger you's help in living most happily and effectively.

As an extension of this activity, ask children to pretend for a while to *be* that younger self and write the you-of-now a letter in return. As with the artworks activity, simply let the writing emerge by itself without trying to control the process. Note that sometimes when you run the activity, some children may notice feelings and memories rising up spontaneously. This is usually a necessary and positive release of emotion.

A variation of the letter-to-self activity is to visit younger-you in the imagination. Imagine a pleasant place where the meeting can take place. Give the younger self some advice and listen to what he/she has to say in return. Offer support and reassurances. Giving a token to each other – some small item – acts as a powerful symbol to consolidate the positive work being done.

■ Positive Platform. Ask children to consider the idea that even emotions that feel unpleasant can serve some positive purpose in your life. Frustration, for example, can indicate a powerful motivation to move on (though you don't have the strategies or a particular direction worked out yet). Disappointment might mean that you care about what has not been obtained or achieved, which in turn allows deeper insight into your personal values. Anger can reflect a sense of injustice, meaning obviously that your strong sense of justice has been outraged. These are a few of many possible interpretations. What feelings mean vary with the individual and are contingent upon particular circumstances.

Note: If you want to learn more about the positive platform idea, a useful book is *The Emotional Hostage* by Leslie Cameron-Bandler and Michael Lebeau (see Bibliography).

■ Gathering Treasures. This is the act of deliberately searching one's memories for positive experiences that help to counterbalance the weight of negative memories you've loaded recently into your mind. For every memory of being worried ask the children if they can find one where they've felt calm, confident, chilled or at least relieved when things worked out OK. Each experience of disappointment can be 'neutralised' with one of achievement. Writing up these positive memories in a journal makes them even more effective and accessible. The gathering treasures technique can be enhanced by DPA. Suggest to the class that from now on children can fully intend to behave with calm confidence, patience, kindness and all the other emotional jewels that are most useful.

■ Mental Mirror. Visualise a mirror around yourself that will reflect any negative thoughts, judgements or feelings you think emanate from other people. The mirror however is cleverly contrived and can allow in 'positive vibes'.[1]

The power of suggestion is also at work here of course, as it is in the other activities we've mentioned. The imagination is powerful. Steve has a friend whose insomnia was completely unaffected by strong sleeping pills. Ben would lie awake at night 'with all kinds of weird and worrying thoughts cycling through my mind'. What cured the problem in the end (believe it or not) was a dreamcatcher. Ben had heard that these trap unpleasant thoughts and dreams and only allow pleasant and positive ones to be noticed. He decided to buy that belief, hung a dreamcatcher near his bed and within days was enjoying night after night of normal, nourishing sleep.

■ The Hourglass of Now. The book by Eckhart Tolle, *The Power of Now*, makes the point beautifully. Imagine an hourglass with sandgrains falling steadily from the future to the past through the 'waist' of the hourglass, which is the present moment. Nobody knows what that future will bring or how many grains are left, and no one can affect the sand that has already fallen. Our only point of influence, one grain at a time, is now. That realisation, imagined as vividly as possible, begins to hand control back to the conscious self embedded in its immediate circumstances. Draw the hourglass and sandgrains falling through the 'waist' one at a time. Ask children to think about the idea that neither the past nor the future exist in such a 'real' and immediate way. Being determined to seize the moment rather than letting the imagination dwell on negative memories or possibilities effectively brings control back to the individual's conscious choice.

As well as the techniques above, others such as learning greater control over one's breathing, progressive muscle relaxation, meditation etc. are also easy to implement and often prove effective.

We also want to mention finally that most of the activities we've suggested work just as well if there are obvious external reasons for anxiety (or whatever the problem might be).

If Jane for instance realised that she was anxious because of relationship problems or money difficulties, she could help herself to respond more positively in the ways we've outlined *and* make conscious, logical and practical decisions in seeking help to resolve the issue. Learning to think towards a solution in this way lies at the heart of what coaching can achieve.

5

Key principles

The following key principles help to create a robust platform for the development of coaching skills and emotional resourcefulness more generally. Considering them as an active force in your thinking (rather than simply as abstract concepts) will support and empower the creative attitude we have already looked at.

The principle of potential

There are many aspects to this idea. One of the most useful is the acknowledgement that we are more resourceful than we realise. Even if there seems to be no way forward, by maintaining the intention to make progress and relying upon our creative abilities (without trying to force answers), any number of possible solutions are likely to emerge.

As a way of introducing this to the children, show them a simple image such as the one below and ask them 'What could this be? What does it remind you of?'

Be prepared for a rush of responses. Typically a class can come up with twenty, thirty or more ideas – It's monkeys' tails. It's a carpet. It's Captain Hook's hook. It's a bunch of question marks. It's a map showing rivers going nowhere. Even if any particular child has only one idea, *all* of the children are exposed to every idea and so all experience the creative act of looking at the image in many ways. Thus, even if implicitly, children come to learn more about the principle of potential.

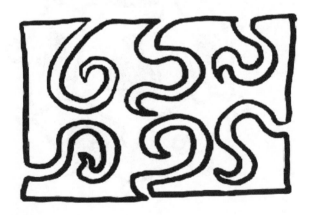

Figure 5.1 Principle of potential

As an extension of the activity ask the following questions –

■   Out of all of the answers I've heard, which is the right answer?

There will usually be several children who say 'Any of them' or 'All of them', to which we reply 'That's very wise'. Then ask –

■   And out of all of the ideas I've heard, which is the best one?

And now, often, even more will say 'Any of them, all of them'. To which we reply…
Because children in schools are expected so often to know 'the right answer' within a competitive and judgmental environment, many find it refreshing to learn that there's another game in town called 'How many ideas can we create and what use can we put them to?'

The principle of purposefulness

This principle presupposes that people's thoughts, feelings and behaviours have an under-lying purpose. Obviously this is an assertion that could be considered controversial and debated at length (alas, something that's beyond the scope of this book), but it has useful applications in developing EI and creativity.
    You might introduce the principle in these ways…

■   If you want to link it with the Principle of Potential, show the children the image below and say 'This is an ancient artefact dug up by archaeologists. It's made of bronze. No one knows quite what it is. What could it have been used for?'

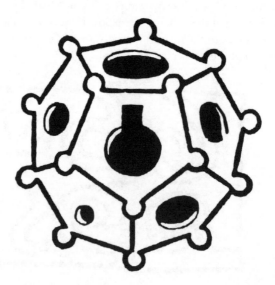

Figure 5.2 Mysterious artefact

The children's ideas now will be influenced by your suggestion that whatever the object might be, it has a purpose. You can repeat the activity any number of times using images and actual objects that you or the children bring in.

- Look at ordinary household objects and discuss why they were designed in a particular way. Whether it's good or bad design, there'll be a reason behind every feature of the item. A linked activity is to explore how structure and function are linked in the natural world – although here the notion of 'design' raises philosophical and religious issues that you may want to avoid. In that case questions can be framed more neutrally – Why is a giraffe's long neck useful? Why do you suppose many butterflies are brightly coloured rather than looking drab? How does a tree shedding its leaves help it to survive?
- Look at the way some poems are set out on the page. We can presume that the poet intended every detail we notice. Similarly all the ideas that go to make up a story have been deliberately worded in a particular way by the author. There is endless scope for asking 'Why might the writer have chosen that word/those words rather than any others?' – or indeed any question that links the author's choices with his/her intentions.

Note: For more detail of 'things happening for reasons' in poems and stories, see Steve's *Countdown to Writing* books and *Developing Literacy and Creative Writing through Storymaking: Story Strands for 7–12 Year Olds* (see Bibliography).

In running such activities as these, although there may indeed be 'right answers', it's useful to keep in mind the notion of 'How many ideas can we have and what use can we put them to?' Also, encouraging children to come up with their own ideas boosts self-confidence and develops their ability to infer, speculate and interpret.

- Revisit the idea of even negative emotions having a positive purpose (see page 23).

The principle of progress

This embodies both a matter of fact and a statement of intent and when incorporated into the creative coaching skill-set puts it a world away from 'hope', which is a rather static and passive view to adopt.

Many fields of human enquiry – from physics to Eastern spirituality – recognise that everything is in a state of motion and flow. It is a basic aspect of human nature that we move onwards on both a societal and personal level. 'Stuckness' and feelings of helplessness or not knowing where to turn are most usually mental constructions – perhaps failures of imagination and nerve (see page 35) – within an individual. Acknowledging the principle of progress begins to build the energy of anticipation and motivates the direct positive action necessary for achievement.

- Future Diary. Invite children to write about their successes and aspirations *as though they had already been achieved.* This stimulates preprocessing (subconscious connecting) that might well lead to sudden insights – Eurkea! moments – on 'how to get there'. Consciously recognised strategies can also be constructed through the application of coaching techniques.

- Timestrips. A variation on the future diary activity is to give each child a long strip of paper and have them mark it off into sections. Each section or box represents a 'step along the road' towards some clearly defined goal. Children can locate themselves anywhere along the strip – although if a child wants to begin in box 1, ask the child to consider what progress he or she might already have made, perhaps without even realising it. When a child recognises 'Oh, well yes I've already done such and such', it acts as a powerful motivator for further progress to be made. You can encourage playfulness with the timestrip idea. Have children identify a goal and then jump into a box in the middle of the strip. What steps could already have been taken to reach that point? What now needs to be done to achieve success?

- Benchmarks. This technique simply amounts to a realisation that progress has been made in a certain area. A simple example would be to ask a child to look back through his or her exercise book and notice how much improvement has occurred in the meantime. This might be in terms of greater understanding of the subject matter, more sophisticated use of language etc. Other benchmark projects that are easy to set up include the group completion of a jigsaw puzzle, with photographs taken regularly as it moves towards completion / collecting stamps, tokens etc. for some charitable cause / growing plants.

The principle of patience

Although Steve risks being labelled a grumpy old man (Simon is anything but, of course), he does tend to think that all too often progress is confused with speed. Fast food appears quickly, but its other virtues might not compare favourably with those of meals prepared from scratch and at greater leisure. There's also the issue of how quickly a meal is eaten – do you for instance rush through your lunch (or miss it out altogether) because you have so many other things to do? And do you savour each mouthful or barely notice the flavours?

This is simply one example of course; it allows Steve to mount his hobby-horse and amble slowly along on it. For many more instances of the damaging effects of the so-called 'cult of speed' see Carl Honoré's *In Praise of Slow* (see Bibliography).

Quite apart from the other aspects of the issue, speed is sometimes linked with impatience – the need to get things done now. This has implications for developing creativity and getting the most out of the coaching process. Although the mind works quickly and is highly efficient at assimilating information, complex tasks take time. (The Belgian mathematician Henri Poincaré's definition of the creative process lists 'incubation' as the stage prior to that of 'illumination', when insights occur and breakthroughs are made.)

Slowing down brings physical benefits in terms of heart rate and pace of breathing, but the mind also quietens. It doesn't necessarily become passive or sluggish, but rather becomes more attuned to small, subtle or fleeting impressions that ordinarily we might miss. Applying the slow-it-down technique in the classroom works best if you've tried it yourself first. If you allow yourself just ten minutes of slow time a day (without watching the clock!), within a week you'll probably look forward to these brief sessions and relish them. In helping children to apply the principle of patience in their creative coaching work, you might try the following…

- Start with short periods of slow-it-down and gradually increase the time; perhaps from a few minutes to five, to ten, or even longer if possible.
- Give the children something to do in the sessions: noticing their own breathing, looking at a painting or photograph, listening to some appropriate background music (not thrash metal), watching the world go by beyond the window.
- Combine slow-it-down with the idea of active meditation.
  - Ask the children to look at, touch, smell and eat a piece of fruit and take ten minutes over it, savouring each moment.
  - Read aloud a short poem (haiku are great for this) or short descriptive passage for the simple pleasure of hearing the flow of words rather than trying to work out any meanings.
  - Have children do some simple act like sharpening a pencil – but slowly.

The principle of positivity

All of the above principles contribute to the Principle of Positivity, which expresses itself in an upbeat outlook and the clear intention that progress will be made and desired outcomes will ensue. Maintaining such a perspective takes practice if it's not already in place. A useful activity for increasing the flexibility of children's thinking (and attendant feelings) is the Fortunately-Unfortunately game.

Start with a simple statement such as 'Mr. Smith was walking down the street'. Then say 'And fortunately…' and invite ideas – It was a lovely sunny day / He met his best friend / He was in time to catch the post etc. Take any of the ideas and say 'So (for example) it was a lovely sunny day, but unfortunately…' – It started to rain / Mr. Smith got knocked down by a mad cyclist / He lost his wallet etc. Take one of those ideas and say 'Mr. Smith lost his wallet. But fortunately…'

And so the game proceeds from there. What children experience – in an atmosphere of fun and creative play – is the ability that the mind has to flip between two viewpoints quickly and easily. It also demonstrates the fact that a positive alternative is almost always imaginable.

If you play the game a number of times, it helps establish a mental technique called 'flipping the coin'. This requires the metacognitive ability to catch yourself thinking a negative thought. As soon as that happens, immediately think the positive opposite. You don't necessarily have to believe it, but it does tend to neutralise the habit of drip-feeding negative impressions into the reactive subconscious.

6

Developing resourcefulness

The word 'resource' is normally used as a noun, but turning it into a verb provides a fresh insight. To 're-source' means to go back to the source; for our purposes, the source of our ability to think. We've already tried to emphasise the importance of creativity in thinking, the capacity we can have to make useful connections and look at things from multiple perspectives. Developing these aspects of creativity keeps thinking flexible and fresh while also supporting the use of so-called 'critical thinking skills'. These ways of thinking rely upon our conscious intelligence; our ability to reason, reflect, discriminate, speculate, infer, consider options, make judgements and reach conclusions prior to making decisions on which we can act. Although distinctions are sometimes drawn between creative and critical kinds of thinking, in practice they are as intertwined and mutually necessary as the elegant lobes of the Yin Yang symbol.

Figure 6.1 Yin Yang

All of our thinking, however, originates from the even more fundamental resources of memory, imagination and experience.

Memory

As we go through life we hear millions of sounds, see millions of images and think millions of thoughts. Consciously much of this is forgotten, but subconsciously these experiences are laid out as a kind of 'map of meaning'. This is sometimes called the map of reality, although like any map it is not the territory itself but rather a representation – our individual interpretations of what we think the world is like and how we fit into it.

And while our maps of meaning influence (and are influenced by) our sense of who we are, our values and beliefs, they are not carved in stone but 'written in patterns of thought' embodied in the neural pathways of the brain. As such we can re-source our memories in all kinds of ways to allow us to survive and to flourish.

Imagination

This is the astonishing power we have to construct mental scenarios that are independent of our immediate circumstances. So for instance as I write this, outside I see freezing fog and snow lies stubbornly on the ground. But by an effortless act of imagination I can conjure up a vision of a tropical beach; white sand, flawless blue sky, warm sun and a sea of the most beautiful aquamarine lapping lazily onto the shore.

The point to be made is that as I used my imagination in this way, I was soothed by the gentle wind, I could smell the sweetness of the air laced with a salty tang: I started to physically relax and for a few moments actually seemed to *feel* the warmth of sunlight on my skin. Also I forgot about the cold grey day outside my window – until my attention returned to it. Even such a simple game of let's pretend demonstrates the fact that each of us is a unity – thoughts, feelings and physical reactions acting as one.

Experience

The etymology of this word is interesting. Experience – from the Latin 'to try' or attempt, but also having links with the Old English *faran*, 'to go' and linking back to the Greek *peran*, 'to pass through'; *poros*, 'a journey'. These are metaphors of movement and travel, of processes rather than states (which are static or 'stuck'). It is also useful to bear in mind the old wisdom that experience isn't so much what happens to us, but what we *make* of what happens to us: how we choose to use what we meet on the journey.

The triangle of failure – or success

Sometimes people are prevented from moving forward because of what they (or others) perceive to be a failure of capability. This may sometimes be true, but equally the obstacle can be a lack of imagination and / or a lack of nerve.[1]

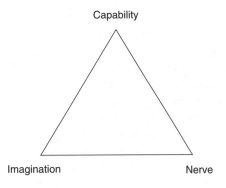

Figure 6.2 Triangle of failure

Failure of imagination is an 'I can't' state, where progress is hindered because the individual simply can't, for whatever reason, envisage the positive outcomes she desires. This may well be based on memories of past failures, or possibly lack of experience in using the imagination as described above.

Simply encouraging the individual to try harder isn't likely to help. Sheer effort could simply be motion without direction: the strategies for *how* to try might be absent. It's like the old idea, 'If the only tool you've got is a hammer you treat every problem as a nail'. Trying to hit something that isn't a nail harder than before probably won't lead to success.[2]

A failure of nerve is an 'I daren't state', again arising possibly from previous negative experiences but exacerbated now by imagined future scenarios of disappointment, humiliation, the negative judgements of others and so on. The famous technique of acknowledging the fear but going ahead anyway might be just the right approach for some people, but anathema to others.

When problems are addressed at this level, the triangle often becomes one of success as capability manifests itself.

A few simple activities for transforming the triangle are –

- Ride a Giant Butterfly. This is an easy visualisation game which the Queen of Wonderland, who has believed as many as six impossible things before breakfast, would approve of. Think of a number of enjoyable and fantastical scenarios and have the children imagine them one at a time. Encourage multisensory thinking – sights, sounds, smells, textures – and suggest that a scenario can be first person or third person. In other words, if you asked children to pretend they were riding a giant butterfly, get them first to imagine it 'through their own eyes' as though they were actually astride the butterfly. Then suggest that they can 'look across or down' at themselves and observe their ride from the outside. A few 'let's pretends' that classes have enjoyed are…
    - Let's pretend snow is warm and all the colours of the rainbow.
    - Let's pretend you can fly like Superman.
    - Let's pretend you are the whole Earth, alive and slowly turning in space.
    - Let's pretend you are walking on the moon. (You will of course need to demonstrate the astronauts' bunny-hop.)
    - Let's pretend you're in Jurassic Park and can talk with the dinosaurs (even the 'raptors).

Although such a game might seem a little frivolous, you are implicitly addressing failures of imagination (and probably nerve) in some children, while working on the metacognitive abilities of the whole class. Also, such acts of imagination are creative insofar as they prompt unusual connections, encourage envisioning situations that don't (and can't) be created using 'routine thinking skills', and thus help to develop the flexibility of thinking needed to generate and consider scenarios from many viewpoints.

Another and equally important function of imagining fantastical experiences is that they may contain important symbolic or metaphorical meanings for a child – as indeed all good myths, legends and fairytales probably do. The 'language' of the subconscious is highly visual and deeply (and personally) symbolic. This, combined with children's natural tendency to 'narratise', to invent tales, forms a bridge between simply making up impossible fictions and rehearsing roles, rights, responsibilities and reasons in the safe environment of a story.

There is also always the potential that even brief visualisations may resonate at a sub-conscious level and lead to a shift of outlook. Steve once met a Y5 child whose self-confidence increased after he'd imagined himself as a football that grew wings and flew over a high brick wall. Previously he had only ever constructed the scenario of himself failing to kick the ball high enough (see page 80).

There is a rich and vigorous growth in the field of 'therapeutic metaphors' and 'healing tales'. A few books we'd recommend are –

- *The Magic of Metaphor* by Nick Owen
- *Stories for the Third Ear* by Lee Wallas
- *How Stories Heal* (audio CD) by Pat Williams.

And those of you who teach very young children might find rich reward in Vivian Gussin Paley's work:

The Boy Who Would Be a Helicopter: The Uses of Storytelling in the Classroom.
- Look Around. This simply involves raising children's awareness that everything they see about them in the classroom was an idea before it could be realised (made real). We say to children, with complete sincerity, 'Look at that window! How can glass be made so clear and in such large sheets? That's wonderful'. Or 'Look at this paper. I wonder how it was invented? And I wonder what the world would be like without it?' You can focus the activity more specifically on themes or subject areas by beginning with the question 'Where has (art and design/maths/science/English/ICT) helped in this classroom?'

Such a game stimulates questioning and encourages an active search for information, while emphasising the positive qualities of a sense of wonder. The game can act as a pre-cursor to: –

- Creative Connections. We'll use Figure 1.1 for this (page 6), although any collection of images will do. This is a brainstorm / free association game where you tell the children that they are going to come up with some new inventions. One good way of doing this is to link two of the images. Here are some examples.
  - Helmet and compass – a SatNav built into a hat and / or spectacles that will help you to find your way around town.
  - A pencil that helped you learn to write as you spoke the words.
  - Bricks and puzzle pieces – interlocking bricks that didn't need mortar.
  - Magnifying glass and footprints – glasses that helped you follow glowing paths along the road and pavement to any place you wanted to go.

One of our favourite creative connections came from a boy, aged about nine, who said 'Gun and hourglass. A gun that doesn't fire straight away – it gives you time to decide if you really want to do it'.

Another trick for making such links is the Merlin Technique – see page 51.

Raising self-awareness

It was Plato who said 'know thyself'; such apparently simple wisdom and yet it begs the question of how well any of us do or can truly have insights into who we are. Not that we should be daunted in any way from trying to find out more. In fact if we accept the idea that greater awareness leads to deeper understanding and that increased understanding leads to greater self-control (of our thoughts, feelings and behaviours), then the task of raising self-awareness can bring rapid and valuable benefits.

In helping children to 'be nosy' about themselves it's important to stress that if any child starts to feel uncomfortable in any activity, then she always has the option of stopping. In Steve's work as a hypnotherapist he sometimes meets people who are frightened to find out 'who they really are' or nervous of what they might discover about themselves. These are valid concerns of course and Steve is always keen to reassure a client that – in the words of Captain Kirk as he leaves the bridge – 'You have the con'. He also suggests that in the vast majority of cases people are their own best friends. Even apparently unhelpful or negative behaviours usually exist for reasons connected with helping the individual to deal with life. That said, while the aim is to enable children to empower themselves through greater self-knowledge and insight, if at any time a child doesn't want to continue then his / her wishes must be respected.

Catch yourself on

A man walks into a post office to send off a package. The place is busy and there's a long queue at the counter. He is annoyed. He has better things to do and his time is being wasted. He stands in line and grows more frustrated, perhaps even muttering just loud enough for people nearby to hear his complaints. After five minutes he's had enough and strides out in a temper...

In this scenario the man may or may not recognise that he is annoyed – in the sense of 're-cognising' or bringing into conscious awareness the fact of his annoyance. In Ireland the phrase 'catching yourself on' means precisely that, to understand what the situation is and why one behaves in a particular way (or at least realising that one *is* behaving in that way). The simple act of noticing creates the opportunity to consider different options...

The options hand

Offer a scenario such as the one above to the children. Ask them to imagine that it rests in the palm of their open hand. Tell them that each finger represents a different way that the man might react to the situation. Ask for suggestions. So…

- He might look on the bright side. 'At least it's warm and dry in here and I'm out of the rain'.
- He might think about other possible reasons for his annoyance. Maybe his boss at work has irritated him today.
- He might 'watch himself being annoyed', just as you might watch a squirrel scurrying about in a tree (the 'detached observer' reaction).
- He might compare himself to other people who are in worse situations. 'I don't like standing here, but look at that old lady. She's bent over and has to use a stick. She looks very uncomfortable'.
- He might simply decide not to be annoyed.

This final option is interesting. It can be an enlightening and also surprising experience simply to decide to feel differently, and then it happens. Newton's third law does not apply to emotional reactions – while it's possible to have a disproportionately negative reaction to a trivial incident, with experience of 'self-management' one can learn to respond more positively and helpfully even in relatively serious or unpleasant circumstances (see Scenario Cards below.)

Scenario cards

Ask the children to write out everyday scenarios such as the post office incident on cards. You then have a resource that you can then use to practise the options hand technique. Extend the activity by putting one such scenario on the board and mind mapping® further ideas.[1] So for instance you can collect other scenarios linked by the 'theme' of annoyance. Or children might offer information on how they would react or have reacted in the same or similar situations. Gathering ideas in this way helps children to name emotions more precisely; thus they may conclude that 'annoyance' is a more accurate description than anger or rage. Also by looking at scenarios like these children have the opportunity to think in advance about how they could respond, underpinned by the now-explicit understanding that options are usually if not always available.

Naming emotions

Use a thesaurus to collect names for a range of feelings. Write each name on a different piece of paper or card.

- Categories. Ask the children to sort the feelings into positive and negative.
- Gradations. Have groups grade emotions in terms of intensity or 'frequency' (how common is that emotion?). If you want children to plot intensity and frequency, they can use a template such as Figure 7.1. You can also add a further dimension by asking

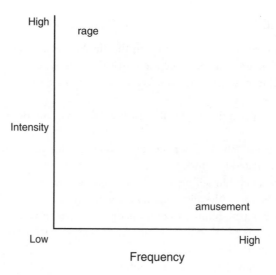

Figure 7.1 Mapping emotions

the children to physically arrange themselves into a continuum and mime the emotion.

■ Matching. Use a scenario card and ask children to match it with an emotion card. You can ask for the emotional responses that children would actually bring to that incident and/or invite suggestions for more helpful or appropriate reactions.

How does it feel?

Ask children to remember an emotion and to describe in detail what it feels like. Ask for physiological detail – my heart beat faster, my breathing was shallower, my shoulders were tense etc. Such increased awareness of how the body responds in the presence of an emotion helps people to 'recognise the signs' as they appear and deliberately change those responses that are under voluntary control. One can choose to untense the shoulders, slow the breathing and so on (with the likelihood that involuntary aspects of the reaction will change as a consequence).

Emotion circles

Represent different emotions as circles of different sizes. The circles can be coloured in or otherwise drawn on – or made from different kinds of material. One class we worked with used sandpaper for aggression (abrasiveness), a velvet-like cloth for gentleness etc. ask children to use the circles as they explore feelings in various ways...

■ Overlap. How does it feel when two emotions overlap? For instance, in the middle of anger seeing the funny side of the situation and breaking into giggles? Ask children to experiment with emotion overlaps and describe their feelings in detail (including the physiology.)

■ Circle Flip. Glue two circles together, faces up. Ask children to match a negative feeling with a positive one that they would prefer to experience. Instruct them to practise flipping the disc negative to positive, first in actuality and then mentally. Encourage the children to concentrate as they carry out the mental disc flip a certain number of times or for a certain length of time. Suggest that when a situation arises when the negative emotion would have appeared automatically, they now have the choice of flipping it to the desired positive response. This technique becomes more powerful over time and works especially well when children have learned to 'catch themselves on'.

■ What would they say? Use a scenario card and group expected or possible emotional responses (emotion circles) around it. Tell the children that each emotion is being experienced by a different person. Ask the children to discuss what each person in the scenario might say. Initially a single comment will do. Subsequently you might want groups to role play the situation and build a dialogue.

Tip: Role play can evoke real emotions, so have the children do it in a designated space, with the option of stepping out of that space whenever they want to. Suggest that stepping out will 'switch off' the feelings that they were starting to experience.

If I were...

Steve once wrote a poem called *If I Were a Spider* that helped 5–7-year-olds to explore aspirations and capabilities...

If I were a spider I'd build a web to the moon.
If I were a sound I'd be a beautiful tune.
If I were a butterfly I'd grow as big as a kite.
If I were a rainbow I'd glow and glitter all night...

The if-I-were idea can be used as a pattern to help children compose their own couplets about what they would like to do or intend to be. With older children the theme or metaphor behind the image can also be made explicit.

If I were a spider – going beyond the given / thinking big ideas / attempting something not because it's easy but because it's hard.

If I were a sound – harmony and discord (dischord?) / orchestration, teamwork, collaboration.

The same idea can 'reframe the metaphor' when it comes to taking a different perspective on feelings, pleasant or otherwise.

If I were joy – I'd shine like the sun on a clear August day.
If I were anger – Like the mist in the morning I'd vanish away.
If I were excitement – A sparrow I'd be.
If I were frustration – I'd set the bird free.

CHAPTER

8

Take responsibility

The primary aims of children learning creative coaching is for them to become more reflective and self-determining, two potential outcomes of being emotionally intelligent. Steve likes to say that someone who can think effectively and apply independence of judgement is 'the captain of his (or her) own ship'. As individuals, however, we are connected in many complex ways to other people. We exist in a variety of contexts, and so the notion of taking responsibility – for one's own actions for instance – must be set against the effects or consequences that will have for others, as well as for ourselves.

The origin and meanings of the word 'responsibility' itself offer a number of useful insights. The Oxford Dictionary suggests that responsibility is acting without authorisation or detailed guidance, in other words the reflective independence of judgement mentioned above. But clearly the word is also linked with 'responsible', which is defined as being morally accountable for one's actions, and capable of rational conduct. There are also connections with 'respond', the etymology of which (from the Latin) is 'to promise in return'.

Another useful idea is to consider responsibility as 'the ability to respond', and since this is a reciprocal act, it must take into account the rights, rules, roles and reasons pertinent to the context where it applies.

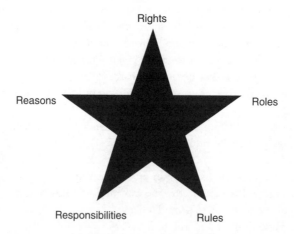

Figure 8.1 The R star

In helping children to understand these various aspects of being responsible, the following activities might be useful.

Right is might

Discuss with the class the rights that people might expect in different circumstances, and how these are bound to generate rules in order for those rights to be enjoyed. Children will doubtless be familiar with school rules. This could be a good time to examine them and look at the reasons and rationales behind them.

On a grander scale, look perhaps at the Universal Declaration of Human Rights and how rights are embodied in national constitutions and in law. Link the notion of rights with laws, rules and regulations. There are opportunities here for discussing the implications of accepting or upholding rights within a group. For instance, what does it mean that everyone has the right to 'life, liberty and security of person'? Discuss those terms and how such ideals might be achieved within society. Can the aspiration of ensuring liberty for everyone restrict what people can do in society?

New world

Ask the children to imagine that they are a group of colonists on a new planet. They can build their society from scratch, and one of the first jobs is to agree on a list of rights that will help the new community to flourish. As the list is generated, ask the class what laws need to be created to ensure those rights – and how those laws might be enforced (sanctions and punishments).

The R-star

Use Table 8.1 to help children to consider how particular rights, roles, rules, responsibilities and reasons are connected. So for instance if a child in class has the right to say 'I don't understand',[1] then it might look like this.

The If-then Game

This activity explores causes, effects and consequences. Launch the game by choosing an if-then scenario and inviting children to respond. Pick one response and turn it into the next if-then. Continue the activity for a certain length of time or until the game seems to have run its course as ideas peter out.

Tip: Even apparently frivolous scenarios have great learning value. In the example below for instance children were (more or less implicitly) making real connections between wealth, leisure, property, land and power. If-thens such as this also build in the 'giggle factor'. When children are enjoying themselves, they tend to be less inhibited in making a response.

- If money grew on trees then people who had no trees would have no money.
- If poor people had no money then they might steal from the rich.
- If the poor stole from the rich then they'd be put in jail.
- If all the poor were in jail those outside would be rich.

Table 8.1 The five Rs

Right - I have the right to say 'I don't understand'.

Role(s)	Responsibilities	Rules	Reasons
Learner	To listen to and think about ideas and explanations	Listen when someone else speaks	It's better to admit you don't understand earlier on than to worry later on
Pupil in a class	To be patient as other people listen and learn	Show respect for other people's ideas	Even if I decide that order ideas are not helpful, thinking about them is still part of my learning

- If all people were rich then there would be no need for them to work.
- If the rich did not work then only the poor could work.
- But the poor could only work if they were not in jail.
- If only the poor worked then they would have to be paid.
- If the poor were paid they might become richer than the rich.
- If the poor became richer than the rich then everyone would be spending a lot.
- If everyone spent a lot then would run out of money.
- If we ran out of money then we would have to plant more trees.
- If we planted more trees then there would be no spare land.
- If there was no spare land then we could not build more houses.
- If we could not build more houses then we would live in the trees.
- If we lived in trees we'd use them as homes instead of for growing money...

'Choice' is a key word when it comes to discussions of responsibility. As was intimated at the beginning of this section, when we choose an action to take we then have to be prepared to accept the responsibility for the outcomes. These may be superficially negative or positive; in other words we should accept praise when it is offered for our actions, and any apparent lack of success is more resourcefully viewed as a learning point from which we can choose another course. As Thomas Edison once remarked on his setbacks when designing a practical light bulb, ' I am not discouraged because every wrong attempt discarded is another step forward.'

Choice and responsibility are important and interlinked concepts in coaching. A coach is not an expert on the coachee, nor every possible goal s/he wants to reach. Coachees are experts on themselves, make choices that are motivating and useful to them, take the actions that they deem necessary, accept responsibility for the outcomes and plan their next goals from there. The choice in choosing is also the choice to accept responsibility for the outcomes. This is an incredibly empowering cycle.

Empowerment here might usefully be linked into a person's 'locus of control' (Rotter, 1954) and how they choose to approach life. This psychological concept refers to the extent to which people consider they control what happens in their lives. Those with a high *internal* locus of control believe that they have significant influence over their own experiences; those with a high *external* locus of control believe that things happen *to* them and that they have little or no influence (i.e. the locus – Latin for 'place' – lies outside of their control, e.g. fate controls their lives). Interestingly, research by Jean Twenge *et al.* (2004) found that American college students in 2002 had a more external locus of control than 80 per cent of students in 1962. It makes us wonder how far these results are representative of the situation in our own and similar cultures and what the causes are. As an external locus of control is associated with negative outcomes, such as underachievement at school, feelings of helplessness and depression, we believe it is important that children be helped to take more control of their lives and move themselves towards a more internal position along this continuum.

Consider one likely outcome of the move to a more external locus of control – the increase in people suing others for their accidents. Though we are sure that there will be times when legal action is required, other instances seem to be about blaming (and claiming money from) others. Who do the children think should accept responsibility in the following examples and why?

- A businesswoman trips over a broken paving stone and twists her ankle.
- A car brakes suddenly because a man steps off the pavement as he is walking along. The man is untouched, but a van runs into the stopped car.
- A house buyer goes to look at the progress of her new house as it is being built. She goes onto site without a protective helmet, despite passing a sign that tells all visitors to put on a hard hat. She trips and bangs her head on some brickwork, cutting her head open.
- A car drives over a pothole and damages its wheel and suspension.
- A child jumps onto a chair in class. The teacher tells her to get down before she falls. She falls and breaks her arm.
- A man goes to the dentist for bridges and crowns to improve the appearance of his smile. He is not happy with the results.

What would make the children change their mind about their verdict (if anything), the age of the person, if the injured had been warned beforehand?

Here are some activities to explore choice, responsibility and control.

- Remote Control. Go out into the playground, pair up the children and ask them to choose who will be 'the controlled' and who will be 'the controller'. Place a row of items at the other end of the playground (anything that is easy to carry, one per pairing) and check that there are no obstacles between the children and the objects.

Turn all the 'controlled' children away from the objects and blindfold them. The controllers must now give instructions to their partner for them to collect any object and return with it to the starting line. The controller may walk next to their partner, but must not touch them. This can be done as a race (without running, of course!), or the game may even be done without blindfolds. Most importantly for any of these, however, is that there is a debriefing session afterwards: How did the controlled child feel not being allowed to make their own decisions? If they had no blindfold, how frustrating was it for them to not do what they wanted to do without being told?

■ Captain of the (Star)ship. Put a creative spin on the choose-your-own-adventure idea by providing a scenario with possible choices for the captain to take. Each choice will lead to further events that allow the class to continue 'writing the story' collaboratively. Set it up as follows: divide the class into small groups, ensuring that there is an even number of groups. Half of the groups will be Story Creators and the other half will be Story Shapers (see Figure 8.3).

A group of Creators must be paired with a group of Shapers. The Creators will be the ones deciding what will happen for each of the options (before it is chosen). The Shapers are the ones choosing and justifying which course they will take. The majority of the group should agree with the choice and one of them will also chart the story – perhaps as an annotated flowchart. To begin, introduce the scene to the class and provide three

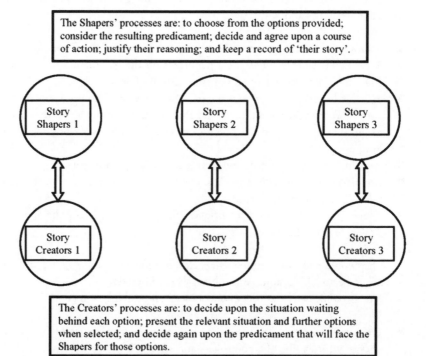

The Shapers' processes are: to choose from the options provided; consider the resulting predicament; decide and agree upon a course of action; justify their reasoning; and keep a record of 'their story'.

Story Shapers 1

Story Shapers 2

Story Shapers 3

Story Creators 1

Story Creators 2

Story Creators 3

The Creators' processes are: to decide upon the situation waiting behind each option; present the relevant situation and further options when selected; and decide again upon the predicament that will face the Shapers for those options.

Figure 8.2 Captain of the starship

options from which the Shapers should choose one. In the meantime, the Creators should be given a sheet explaining what will happen for each option chosen. This will serve as an example for what they will be doing in the next round. When the Shapers choose their option, their partner-group of Creators can explain what happens next on their particular route through the story. This explanation will end with two options, for which the Creators will devise outcomes and two further choices (though they need not consider the scenarios for those yet). We would suggest a set time on a visible timer for each segment. Further activities from this include (for Shapers) telling their story, dramatising it for performance (audio or visual); (for Creators) design and lay out an adventure book based on the activity, or prepare instructions and a flowchart for others wishing to undertake this game.

Here is an example scenario of many you could use:

An enemy battle fleet has arrived and your ship is down to 50 per cent power with the nearest reinforcements several Earth hours away. You have casualties on board as well as an important passenger whom the other side would like to question, though your enemy has a reputation for being brutal. Surrender is an option. There is a planet within teleporting distance (ten could go at a time and there are 34 of you, including wounded) and an uncharted wormhole you have located to which your vessel should be able to jump before the enemy reacts. Will you opt to surrender (reason: you might be used in a prisoner exchange), begin teleporting (reason: enemy not to be trusted as jailers, so elude them and use survival techniques until rescue arrives) or jump for the wormhole (reason: perhaps the best chance of escape, but literally a leap into the unknown)? (You won't know this when making your decision, but the surrender will result in you and your crew being imprisoned until a slave ship arrives, and your VIP whisked away for 'questioning'; teleporting will be successful for 30 of your crew [which includes all the wounded], but the enemy then remotely jams your equipment and storms the ship to find you and three others left; the wormhole jump is successful, though you are now down to 20 per cent power, not enough to thrust free from the gravitational pull of a planet near to where you emerged. Whichever one of these you chose will also have two or three options to consider to move you into the next scenario.)

For other scenario ideas, including ones from everyday life, please see the website.

http://www.routledge.com/9780415577809/

You may have noticed that, bubbling under the surface, this section suggests some intriguing and exciting questions. What if we all took responsibility for our actions? How would the world change? Go back a few steps…what if it started in your class, spread throughout the school, rippled out into the children's homes, continued into the local community, created a wave across your county, the country…?

9

Building confidence and belief in yourself

It's interesting to note that the word 'confidence' shares its origins with 'confide', from the Latin 'to trust', which itself derives from the Greek term 'to believe'. So significantly confidence amounts to belief and trust in oneself, in the same way that self-esteem at its heart is how we estimate *ourselves* – though ironically for many people their sense of self-esteem is based on the judgements and opinions of others.

In building self-confidence and self-belief then, Plato's encouragement to 'know thyself' has a further resonance. As we help children work towards this goal, perhaps as adults we might consider a number of key ideas –

■ Beliefs grow out of values.[1] What we value creates an emotional platform on which we stand as we look out upon and walk in the world. The mythologist Joseph Campbell has repeatedly and eloquently discussed the noble qualities of the hero and that which he values; courage, altruism, loyalty, determination and more (an Internet search on 'the qualities of a hero' will throw up many other fascinating ideas!). Campbell has also said that the difference between a hero and celebrity is that a hero's actions are motivated by consideration of others, whereas a celebrity's actions are motivated by consideration for him/herself.

■ Cockiness is not confidence. Achievement (as determined by oneself and/or others) is its own reward that can bring a quiet pleasure rather than the need to brag. It is indeed true that arrogant people might well be talented, but their achievements and successes are their own testament which boastfulness diminishes.

■ Comparisons are odious – but are they inevitable? Comparing oneself to others has probably always been a human tendency, but it can be damaging if a child already feels that s/he is lacking in some way. What might the consequences be if the child thinks that s/he is not as attractive or clever or wealthy or successful as his/her contemporaries? And what societal/cultural forces have inspired that thought? Among the negative effects we find –

　■ Wishful Thinking. The yearning to be different or better, or to be like someone else. Such 'if only' thinking fuels the fires of dissatisfaction and can lead to disappointment, jealousy, frustration and anger.

　■ Generalising. Turning a single negative event (perhaps some personal shortcoming or mistake) into a general opinion or belief about oneself. Other incidents that are at all similar may be added to the toxic mix and so increase the tendency towards such a limiting habit or compulsion of thought.

- Negative Filtering. This is the tendency to select out from one's experiences only those aspects that support general self-limiting beliefs. Eventually such beliefs may become ossified or frozen (a state known as 'hardening of the categories') and form the basis of unshakeable conclusions – I'll never succeed at this / I'll never be as good as so-and-so / I'm a loser.
- Mind Reading. Assuming (and fearing) that you know what someone else is thinking or feeling about you, and using this to reach negative conclusions. This habit of thought may lead to the similar so-called 'cognitive distortion' of fortune telling, where unhelpful predictions are made about future events. The dangers of fortune telling are that you can begin to behave as though these unfortunate consequences had already come about, and so increase the likelihood of turning into a self-fulfilling prophecy.
- Emotionally Weighted Reasoning. Assuming that your negative perceptions reflect the world as it really is. As the saying goes, an angry man lives in an angry world.
- 'Should' Limiters. The word 'should' is limiting because it often invites negative comparison or judgements, and feelings of guilt through inaction. It is usually attached to 'but' (which may be implicit) and that serves to highlight the fact that nothing has been done. Sticking 'and so' can lead to negative conclusions – 'I should have tidied my room but I didn't, and so I'm just lazy'. The should-but-so pattern is one of the most dangerous in the language, along with 'they say'.
- Competitiveness is but one tool in the toolbox. Perhaps we've all heard the saying 'We live in a competitive society'. But what does that actually mean? Pitting ourselves against others to test our abilities is useful and pleasurable in some contexts but not others. Sport is the obvious example where competition is not only the driving force among the competitors, but the *raison d'etre* for the activity itself – and the enjoyment it brings. The world of business is another field in which competition enters into the equation (whether for good or ill or both being open to debate). However, the concept of competitiveness is meaningless, limiting or downright dangerous in other areas. Although competitiveness and the comparisons it brings is a significant aspect of our educational system, one might question whether its general application here does more harm than good as far as some children are concerned.[2]

One way of helping your class to appreciate that competitiveness is a tool that serves some purposes well and others poorly is to discuss with them statements such as these –

- The richer you are the happier you are.
- I can run faster than you so I'm better than you are.
- I'm happier than you are.
- There will always be people who can do things better than I, and those who aren't as good as I.
- I scored higher in my latest maths test so I've become better at maths.
- Ben Leech has written more books than Philippa Stephens and so he's a more successful author.

- Attainment and achievement are not identical. This idea was brought home to Steve when a teacher he met asked his class to give some thought to a question he posed and write a page about it. 'I'm interested to know what you think, so find a quiet spot to mull it over and then jot down your ideas'. Next day David handed in a few lines of barely legible script on a scrappy piece of paper – and his teacher was delighted (whereas Steve's knee-jerk reflex was to think that David's was rather a poor effort). Later the teacher explained that David was the oldest of five children and spent much of his time looking after them. He lived in cramped conditions with Mum and siblings, his father having walked out some time ago. 'To get any writing at all out of him pleases me', the teacher said. 'He has such difficulty putting pen to paper. In any 'objective' test he would score low on attainment, but his achievement in producing this is great'.

In helping children to raise their levels of confidence and self-belief, these activities may be useful –

- Positive Purpose. We've already looked at the idea that even negative and unpleasant emotions can serve a positive purpose (page 23). So envy for instance, while it might simply intensify the emotions associated with wishful thinking, could with imagination and nerve become a positive energy prompting action to achieve one's desires. See also the flipping-the-coin technique on page 49.
- Anchoring. Creating a link between positive empowering feelings and something you have under your own conscious control. So for example, when you do something with confidence / that pleases you / that elicits sincere praise, carry out some small movement or gesture to create a link. One example of such an anchor is to rub the thumb and little finger of the left hand together (if you're right handed). This movement isn't likely to be done accidentally, but is a deliberate connection between *that* movement and *those* feelings. The anchor is cumulative, so if you teach it to children encourage them to notice occasions when it's appropriate to develop it (This in itself will prompt 'positive filtering', noticing only those incidents that fit with the link that's being strengthened.) When the anchor is established, use it in situations when you might otherwise feel negative; upset, disappointed, envious etc. Firing the anchor now tells the brain, as it were, to generate positive feelings even under these circumstances. Anchoring can be used with various other of the cognitive techniques mentioned in this book.

Note: Anchoring is an idea often found in the field of NLP (neuro-linguistic programming), together with many other techniques pertinent to the aims of this book. A good introduction is O'Connor and Seymour's *Introducing Neuro-Linguistic Programming* (see Bibliography).

- Gathering Treasures (see also page 23). This is simply the act of noting occasions when something is done with kindness, generosity, friendship etc. or when something is achieved. The gathering treasures activity can take various forms –
  - Encourage children to keep a diary of even the smallest of their achievements (regardless of attainments).

- Positive Post-it Board. Ask children to notice when others are kind to them and to write their appreciation on a sticky notelet, which is then posted on a display board. You might drop in the suggestion of wondering how quickly the class can fill that board.
- Look on the Bright Side Hats. Use actual hats if you like. When a child wears such a hat s/he must notice and talk about something positive seen in others, in his or herself, about the way the day is going etc.

10

Improving decision making

We've already advocated the DPA (direct positive action) approach to developing emotional resourcefulness – the idea that doing something is better than doing nothing. It's the difference between motion and direction; in this instance 'motion' being the energy we expend worrying, feeling frustrated, feeling helpless or stuck etc. There is a distinction to be made, however, between doing *anything* and doing something that's effective. In order to make decisions that are more likely to be helpful to us, we can call upon the range of thinking skills we have at our disposal. For convenience these are usually separated into the so-called critical kinds of thinking and the creative kinds (although in our opinion this is an artificial and simplistic distinction. Minds operate in an 'all-at-once-together' way such that logical reasoning supports and is supported by the fuzzier thinking we call intuition, hunches, gut feelings and so on.)

Critical thinking (critical in the sense of analytical) operates largely in a conscious way and includes the ability to sequence, predict, prioritise, attribute, classify, categorise and deconstruct. These modes of thinking are logical insofar as the outcomes are the result of chains of reasoning that are 'out in the open'. The critical thinking agenda is (ideally) transparent to examination such that anyone can see how a conclusion has been figured out.

Creative thinking as we have seen appears to be less sequential. Unexpected connections are made often subconsciously, so that while the outcomes of creativity burst into consciousness as a Eureka Moment, the processes that lead to it are hidden away and often not amenable to reasoned analysis. It goes without saying that ideas of this kind are no less valid than those that are logically constructed – and in fact their usefulness or veracity is often strengthened by feelings of certainty, that 'yes this is the right thing to do'. As Doctor Who in his second (Patrick Troughton) incarnation said, logic merely allows one to be wrong with authority; so when this possibility looms, the presence of a creative perspective is likely to be valuable.

The 1998 report *All Our Futures: Creativity, Culture & Education* defined creativity as 'Imaginative activity fashioned so as to produce outcomes that are both original and of value'. So the question remains how might we help children to 'fashion' ideas and come to decisions that will be of value to them? Here are a few suggestions.

Coin flip game

It was Edward de Bono (famous for his work on lateral thinking) who suggested that the introduction of randomness and chance encourages creativity and lessens the tendency to rely on 'routine thinking'. Routine thinking amounts to a limited repertoire of strategies whose outcomes are not as diverse or useful as they might otherwise be. This can be summed up in the idea that 'if the only tool you've got is a hammer, you'll treat every problem as a nail'. It is easy to see how coaching might remedy this. When someone takes on the role of coach, part of their 'job' is to help the coachee find new ways forward to the ones that their routine thinking has so far produced. When coaching oneself, creative prompts can help the individual find an innovative route to achieving their goals.

Flipping a coin is a simple and non-threatening way of allowing children to make unexpected connections and generate unanticipated thoughts.

Look back to Figure 1.3 on page 8. Ask children to think of questions about the picture that can be answered yes or no. They can flip a coin to obtain the answers, heads for yes and tails for no. Any reasonable question is allowable. Are the two people married? Is the man a criminal? Is the woman in danger? Have they just robbed a bank? Sequences of questions are likely to be based on a set of assumptions and inferences as the child attempts to create a narrative that makes sense of the picture and creates a broader context. But half of the time the child's train of thought will be interrupted by the coin coming up *no*. So, for instance, if the man is not a criminal (as the child perhaps wanted him to be so that the story would be exciting), then a new idea needs to be framed in terms of a further question based on that answer – while keeping the story just as interesting. There is a useful parallel here to the coaching process; a coach cannot plan questions in advance, as s/he doesn't know (and should not anticipate) what the answers will be. Instead, the coach needs to listen carefully to what the coachee is saying before formulating the next question.

You'll appreciate that playing the coin flip game puts a 'positive pressure' on children to keep coming up with new ideas, built on the increasing resource of information that accumulates as the game progresses. Some children (usefully) develop the knack of asking the same question in different ways so that the coin gives them the outcome they want. (Will the man become a criminal *tomorrow*?) Implicit in this learning is the notion that the way a question is framed often influences the answer that matches it.

You can extend the activity by asking children to assess which questions they found to be most useful. Also point out that many of the answers open the way for more questions to be asked – an important insight when it comes to learning how to make more powerful decisions.

Note: For further ideas on using coin flips in the context of literacy see *Countdown to Creative Writing*.

Problem solver grid

Create a 6 X 6 grid such as Table 10.1. The boxes can contain words, pictures or a mixture. Boxes are chosen randomly by dice rolls. Any item is selected by rolling twice, counting the numbers 'along the corridor and up the stairs', so that a roll of 4/3 will bring us to 'leaves'.

Table 10.1 Problem solver grid

Castle	Shield	Axe	Map	Two Heads	River
Forest	Shackles	Rocks	Flight	Jewel	Threshold
Waves	Hand	Chain	Puzzle	Happy and Sad	Lost
Wolf	Friends	Shooting Star	Leaves	Moon	Season
Mountains	Set	Entrance	Wheat	Guardian	Rock
Storm	Eyes	Dream	Treasure	Imp	Cross

To play the game, tell the children that the words and pictures will help to solve many different kinds of problems. Firstly identify the problem you want to work on. Then suggest that rolling the dice twice to choose an item from the grid 'will tell us something that we didn't know about the problem'. Notice that this instruction is rather vague, even while you are suggesting that the children *will* learn something new. The technique is called 'artful vagueness'. You are combining the expectation of further learning while preventing the use of conscious routine thinking skills, since the box has not yet been chosen. However, the children are likely to be *preprocessing* the grid – subconsciously considering how any number of items offer new information about the chosen problem.

Now roll the dice and gather ideas.

The next step is to say 'Now we'll roll the dice to choose another box and this will give us ideas about solving the problem'. Point out that any ideas are useful at this stage (as in the 'ideas cascade' phase of brainstorming). No judgements are made about the usefulness of the ideas – they all go into the melting pot.

There will probably be a rush of thoughts initially (Eureka moments), then a tailing-off as children try and 'work out' how the item in the box might solve the problem. The best way to deal with this is to move on rather than let children struggle. Say 'We'll roll the dice a third time and this will tell us something new about how we can use the (last item) to help solve the problem'. Children now have another opportunity to make creative links between the three boxes chosen so far.

Follow the question trail

A more sophisticated version of the activity is to keep asking questions that prompt more dice rolls to suggest further insights. Here is a worked example –

Problem: How can I (Steve) get more work done given limited time? (Note that my immediate 'conventional' responses were – prioritise / work smarter not harder. But let's see what the grid turns up…)

1. Roll the dice to choose an item that throws further light on the problem. 3/3 shooting star. My immediate thought was that this problem is a 'flash in the pan' that will soon vanish.

2. This encourages me, but how can I use my time more effectively now when my workload is high? 4/1 treasure. I'm thinking about how precious time is. Also the idea of 'hidden treasure' occurs to me.

3. What might the hidden treasure be that will help me? 3/5 rocks. I think these are obstacles – or maybe I'm just thinking of them as rocks. How else could I view them?

4.   6/6 River. This suggests 'going with the flow'. What does this mean? If I just carry on working as I have been (not slacking but not knocking myself out), I'll get the jobs finished. I've also had the thought that a river flows around rocks and is not interrupted by them. But what might the consequences be if I run out of time?

5.   4/6 Map. My immediate thought is orienteering – orienting myself differently. This reinforces the insight that seeing time as an obstacle is not helpful. I'm also thinking 'co-operate with the inevitable'. I can only do so much.

Playing the game for just a few minutes has already helped me to change my perspective on the issue. While I still have as much to do in the same amount of time, I *feel* differently about it all. But let's say I wanted a couple of (equally?) pragmatic solutions. How for instance could I go about prioritising my tasks?

6.   3/4 Chain. Arrange jobs so that they interlink. Can I organise things so that doing the previous job helps me to complete the next one?

7.   In other words, how can I work smarter in this way? 4/5 flight. Immediate response is 'rise above it all', which helps me to realise that my feelings of pressure and worry are largely self-imposed. In an immediately practical way I'm completing this section of the book more swiftly by revisiting ideas I developed some time ago – the coin flip game for instance, and also the 6 X 6 grid which I devised to help children create stories. If it hadn't been for that earlier thinking, I'd be taking much longer to finish this section off.

Playing the problem solving game is another example of 'going with the flow' and letting ideas pop into mind, once it has been suggested that there are further insights to be had. The answers I have produced are my own, crafted by my own creativity to help me find a way forward, and so demonstrating that I can resolve problems myself. It also requires metaphorical thinking, where the concrete images of chain or rocks or forest represent feelings, issues or abstract concepts. You can easily help children to understand this by asking them to think about the *qualities* of the item chosen. So the qualities of a castle for instance are that it's strong, stands on high ground (with good views), it protects and guards, it keeps the world out, and so on. See also our comments on metaphors on page xx.

The Merlin Game

Another robust strategy for making decisions is the well-known 'Merlin Game'. It's played by firstly identifying the problem: this may mean listing its various factors or components, and then altering them in the various ways mentioned below.

When you run the activity with children, explain to them that Merlin is 'the wizard of your imagination and that by waving his wand he can help you to change the way you look at things'.

The elements of the game are –

■   Make bigger (enlarge)
■   Make smaller (reduce)

- Change shape (transform)
- Take something away (remove)
- Swap (substitute)
- Turn something around (reverse)

Each of these elements encourages a shift of perspective, more flexible thinking and an opportunity to make different connections.

As with many of the creativity techniques in the book, you don't need to work on 'real life problems' as you give children experience in these ways of thinking. In fact choosing fantastical or humorous examples helps to keep the game light, detached as it is from the real world.

So for instance you might use the example of Prince Charming quickly wanting to find the girl whose foot fitted the glass slipper. Ask the children 'To do this, what could he make bigger? What could he make smaller? What could change shape?'

Employ the principle of brainstorming by accepting all ideas without analysing them in any way at this stage.

11

Nurturing a positive outlook

Think highly of yourself, for the world takes you at your estimate.

Anon

With a little thought we can appreciate that an 'outlook' means the way we look out at the world; the viewpoint we choose (or otherwise) to take. Other sections in the book have already touched on this topic, but it's worth developing it further since the idea is central to the effective use of creative coaching skills and will aid in the development of EI.

Reminders: Here are some of the concepts that can support us in nurturing a positive outlook...

- The map is not the territory. Each of us carries a mental 'map' of what we think the world is like and how we fit into it. Much of this map is subconscious (and most of it may never come into conscious awareness normally). However, we draw upon this map (double meaning intended) constantly to make sense of the world moment by moment. The so-called map of reality is not reality as such, but our incredibly complex network of associations and interpretations *about* the world. Such mental structures are ultimately a wonderful resource and are frequently amenable to our conscious influence.

- Perception is projection. Simply put, this is the mental feedback loop which is inevitably established over time. Our map of reality creates perceptual filters that 'colour' our world view such that experiences are interpreted in habitual and particular ways. An angry man lives in an angry world. A happy man encounters happiness constantly. We can of course stick with our 'default' outlook on things (which in the latter case is probably preferable), or choose to do something about it – starting perhaps with the notion that to make progress we can change our circumstances and / or ourselves.

- Cognitive Distortions. This term refers to the ways in which our mental filters colour the world view in an unhelpful or negative fashion. Leaving aside the philosophical question of whether anyone could achieve a 'pure' and 'objective' view of the world, once these habits of thought have been noticed, they can be addressed and corrected to a greater or lesser extent. A very common and pervasive distortion for example is that of 'mind reading' where we make assumptions about what's going on in other people's heads – usually with regard to what they're thinking about us. Thus we can easily form the opinion that we are being negatively judged, when a moment's reflection leads us to realise that we *can't* know in detail what someone else is thinking (despite the more grandiose claims of NLP) unless they tell us. Catching yourself on doing the mind reading habit can bring swift and powerful benefits.

- Principle of Positive Purposes. This is the idea that even apparently unpleasant or negative emotions are 'telling us something' that can be of positive use and value. So for instance our angry-man-in-an-angry-world might reflect on his anger and conclude that it's linked let's say to a sense of injustice. Further reflection might help to unpack the details of this issue, so leading to greater understanding and putting him in a more powerful position to make decisions and act on them. Notice that the anger is not being denied or suppressed, nor are judgements being made about the appropriateness of the anger response. It is being considered as a resource, and a considerable one at that, given how much energy is given over to the maintenance of such an emotion.

- The Power of Now. While we have the ability to remember the past and anticipate the future (this being a gift or a curse, depending on how we use it), for our practical purposes neither the past nor the future exist. Our point of influence lies in the present moment. This is easy to say of course and often hard to apply. Regret, disappointment, anxiety and worry, fearful anticipation and a host of other unpleasant feelings testify to that – and to the strength of our imaginations. But simply to contemplate the notion that the richness of life is most fully appreciated *now* can begin to establish its reality. This in turn acts as a basis for making beneficial decisions and strengthening our positive intentions to act.

Activities

- Mottoes to Live By. Offer children an appropriate motto (or have them choose their own) and encourage them to live by it for a day or so as far as they can. So you might pick 'Treat others as you would like to be treated'.[1] Discuss what it means and its various implications with the class, then suggest that the children go ahead and apply it. Explain that they are giving the motto a 'trial run' and ask them to notice (and perhaps record) their observations and reactions. A variation of the activity is to have the children *imagine* what things would be like if that motto was being applied. In this case, suggest different scenarios and discuss with the class how people might react: create imaginary dialogues, role-play various scenes, etc.

- As If. This activity is a variation of the mottoes game and is linked to the notion of positive affirmations. An affirmation can be defined as a positive statement of intent. Interestingly the word's origins lie with the Latin *affirmare*, 'to make firm'. So an affirmation is not to be regarded as some kind of make-believe[2] or delusion, but a firm basis of decision and intention out of which action arises. One of the most famous affirmations, coined by the psychologist Émile Coué, was 'Every day in every way I'm getting better and better'. Notice the generalised vagueness of this self-suggestion. If acted upon as if it were truly happening, its implications will be assimilated both consciously and subconsciously, leading (one intends) to a new set of helpful filters!

- Positive Journal. Positive changes are more powerful if they are remembered and revisited. In the same way that children can note down the results of the 'gathering treasures' activity (see page 23), so they will benefit from keeping a record of how their thoughts and feelings change, and how this influences other people's reactions, when they nurture a positive outlook. Encourage children to look back through their journals at regular intervals.

- Maybe-Maybe Not. This mental exercise combines the Options Hand (page 35) with Flipping the Coin (page 49) – and of course there's also an element of 'catching yourself on' (page 34). It's dangerously easy to daydream one's way into a negative state. I might be sitting on a bus and notice that one person seems to be staring at me, then another and then another. None of them are smiling and I begin to wonder if maybe they think I'm odd in some way. In fact their expressions look almost hostile. Maybe I've offended them in some way. I start to grow anxious and think about getting off at the next stop to be out of their way – except what if they get off too and come after me!

Although this is a rather dramatic scenario it isn't made up. Steve knew a person some years ago who was becoming increasingly nervous about going out in public because she thought people were staring at her and making negative judgements. She allowed herself to dwell on this idea until it became a firm conviction (she'd made a belief), one that forced her to stay indoors as much as she could and dread those occasions when she had to go out.

Using the maybe-maybe not technique is a simple but effective way of stopping such a downward spiral. So I'm on a bus and notice that a person seems to be staring at me – well maybe, or maybe not. Perhaps he's just gazing vacantly into space, simply daydreaming like I am. Several people look stony faced, even slightly hostile – well maybe, or maybe not. Perhaps they've not had a good day so far, or perhaps they're just unhappy (all for different reasons). At each stage in the (idle) daydream that's leading me towards unpleasant feelings I can catch myself and choose to think of some more positive or at least neutral alternative. Deciding to use the technique –

- Creates greater self-awareness but dampens self-consciousness.
- Keeps thinking flexible and inhibits the tendency towards negative habits of thought.
- Forms a bridge to the use of the 'as if' principle (page 54). I can choose to act as if the people on the bus simply look dour that has nothing to do with myself. I can decide to keep smiling[3]!
- A matter of balance. Both Simon and Steve have run training days where virtually all of the evaluations have been positive, though one or two have been less complimentary. In both our cases the first reaction was to feel hurt and disappointed by the negative comments rather than pleased and buoyed-up by the positive ones. In fact, it's the easiest thing to remain upset by those critical remarks to the point where their negative effect completely outweighs the pleasure we should have taken from the enthusiastic comments we received.

Attempting to 'restore the balance' requires some effort, and sometimes repeated effort, since the tendency to feel bruised in such a way might be the result of a largely subconscious context whose roots go back to one's childhood. Negative remarks by parents, teachers and others might be exerting an influence years later. Teaching children to consciously and deliberately 'weigh up' a situation restores a healthier perspective on events at the time.

Finally, and on a personal note, Steve would like to recommend Dale Carnegie's *How to Stop Worrying and Start Living*. He read this book as a teenager and found it packed with easy, practical tips for developing confidence and beating the worry habit. Also the style is wonderfully upbeat and every section is filled with heartwarming anecdotes.

12

How we shape ourselves

You'll notice the title of this section suggests that it's not a question of if or whether we *can* shape ourselves, but that we inevitably do. More implicitly, that we have a range of options and strategies we may apply to achieve it. It's also the case that such 'shaping' might occur through our inaction; because we aren't motivated to change or perhaps frightened to try, or due to the limiting belief that it's not possible. The same idea is found in the notion that 'evil triumphs when good men do nothing'. If we make no effort towards becoming more self-determining, then our passivity might allow otherwise unwanted influences to affect us.

Much of what we've already looked at in this book serves to prepare the ground for taking direct positive action towards our desired goals. Having imagined these so-called 'well-formed outcomes', and having identified (or suspected) possible obstacles to progress, we can choose which steps to take that will serve us most effectively and beneficially.

The coaching techniques you'll learn in subsequent sections will bring these ideas into sharper focus. For now here are a few broader strategies you can try out with your children.

What we think we know

This is a simple but powerful way of investigating situations. The idea is to apply these three questions to an event, issue or problem –

1. What do we know?
2. What do we think we know?
3. What do we need to ask to find out more (or be sure)?

Look back at Figure 1.3 (page 8) in light of these three questions. The picture of the woman standing outside the window with the man indoors on the phone was used initially to think of alternative scenarios –

- A wife coming home from work finding her husband having an angry phone conversation.
- The man's daughter dropping by unexpectedly after being away for some months.
- The woman walking out on the man because she's tired of his moodiness.

And so on. But now the emphasis is different. What we actually *know* with regard to the picture is limited to a relatively small number of observations...

- There's a car parked right outside the window.
- The woman has a bag over her right shoulder.
- The woman's left hand is raised.
- The man has loosened his necktie etc.

Children usually pick up the knack of playing this game very quickly. The observations above (along with many others) were given by pupils in a Y5 class. But within a few sessions some children were checking back over what had already been said. Their comments included –

- The person standing outside might not be a woman ('Could be a man is disguise' was one suggestion.)
- The object over the 'woman's' shoulder might not be a bag.
- Maybe the man didn't loosen his own necktie. Perhaps someone else did it.

We think this is pretty sophisticated thinking. Many of the children were already noticing how easy it is for us to make assumptions, jump to conclusions and take things for granted. Here the children were 'catching themselves on' when doing this, and correcting themselves in the process.

Once you've established a number of things that you agree to, you *know* about the picture, move on to the second phase and ask the children what they think they know. Some of the things they've already said will fit into this category. This phase offers a good opportunity to revisit ways of thinking the children have met, and introduce new ones...

- Making Assumptions. Assuming is the act of taking something for granted in the absence of evidence, or with minimal evidence. Point out to the class that, for instance, it's a fact that the man's necktie is undone, but we only assume he loosened it himself.
- Drawing Inferences. An inference is a conclusion we come to by drawing together observations and ideas that support it. So although we don't know that the man and woman know each other, we can infer it from the way they seem to be waving at each other.
- The Notion of Reasonableness or Likelihood. This mental 'sliding scale' can be applied to reflect on the relative strengths of the conclusions we reach. It's more reasonable to assume that the people in the picture know one another, than that the woman is a complete stranger passing by and wants to attract the man's attention because she's suddenly fallen in love with him.

Note that reasonableness indicates that reasons must be given to support one's conclusion. In the example above, what reasons could children offer for the greater likelihood that the two people know one another? (We think this task is harder than it first seems!)

Help children to become more familiar with the sliding scale of reasonableness by saying something like, 'One a scale of 1 to 5, the idea that the lady is coming home from work and waving to her partner is 'one'. The idea that she's a neighbour coming to borrow some coffee is also 'one'. If she was a stranger passing by trying to warn him that someone was stealing the wheels off his car, that would be 'two' or maybe 'three'. If she was an enemy spy sent to steal important secrets from him, that's a 'four'. And so on. Once you've offered a few examples, ask the children to give you more – including 'fives', which have to be wacky and off-the-wall.

This game gives children more conscious control over linking decisions to reasons, and helps prevent their imaginations running away with them.

- 'Because' Adhesive. 'Because' like 'therefore', 'so' and 'it follows' are *sticky* words, since reasons need to be stuck to them. The reasons can refer to observed facts, inferences and assumptions. Use what the children have talked about so far to demonstrate the adhesive nature of these connectives.
  - The man is warm because his necktie is loosened.
  - The weather is cold because there is snow on the windowsill.
  - If the car belongs to the lady she has a good job, because a car like that is expensive to maintain.
  - The lady doesn't have a ring on her wedding ring finger, so she isn't married.

Finally, move to the last phase of the three-step investigation and say, 'What do we need to ask to find out more?' The aim of this ideally is to turn assumptions and inferences into further facts, although of course in terms of the picture many of the children's questions will remain unanswered.

Once children have used the three-step approach in this context, apply it in different areas of the curriculum; analysing texts for instance, or science. It is also useful of course in helping children to explore issues related to the whole idea of self-determination.

Narrative template

It seems to be a natural tendency in people to weave together the experiences of life into a kind of story or narrative.[1] In fact the root of the word 'context' and 'text' is shared and means to weave or braid (the word textiles is also related). In fact we talk about one's life story, a new section beginning, and 'turning over a new leaf' or page. Since we normally perceive the passage of time as a linear sequence of events, the matching pattern of a story helps us to make sense of what we experience.

Important work has been done by the folklorist Vladimir Propp in identifying a number of basic elements in narrative structures. These are – Hero, Villain, Problem, Journey, Partner, Help, Power (gained through knowledge) Object.

These important insights can be combined with what is traditionally seen as the fundamental 'shape' or structure of a story (Figure 12.1).

Briefly the ten points on the journey are –

1. The Hero's Call to Action. This is where the hero recognises a problem and realises s/he must do something about it.

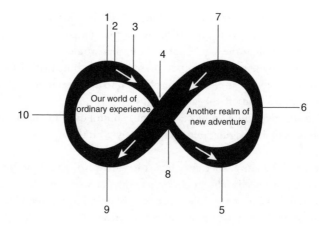

Figure 12.1 Basic narrative template

2.   Often there is a reluctance to set out on the journey, but soon the hero's 'noble qualities' move him or her to act.

3.   A Perception of Danger. Sometimes when we begin to move towards resolving a problem, we feel apprehensive or worry about going into 'uncharted waters'. Such anxiety *may* be justified in terms of real danger, or more likely is the feeling we get as we step out of our comfort zones. For our purposes, such anxiety or fear (see the Triangle of Failure on page 31) can be the villain of the peace. It's the villain who creates problems, but in all good stories that character is defeated by the more powerful hero.

4.   At some point the hero reaches an important threshold. Things might still seem difficult, and the way might be rough, but the hero has been learning new tricks (and rediscovering some old ones) and is powerfully equipped to move into the realm of new experience. Traditionally a guardian figure stands at the threshold and somehow tests the hero. Passing the test (which may mean learning from the mistakes we make) strengthens the hero even more.

5.   We have all felt 'at a low ebb' and been tempted to give up hope, in matters both minor and major. So too with our journey of self-determination we may feel that the task is impossible. But we've come this far and the rewards of our endeavours are great.

6.   At this stage in the journey things might seem to be 'on the up', but the hero must not become complacent. Traditionally this is a point farthest from home, where even small setbacks can seem like major ordeals and the way ahead can feel like an uphill struggle.

7.   But effort pays off. However, life can be a bit of a rollercoaster ride and even though we know we've come a long way and are making progress, ups and downs still continue.

8.   Even though we're well on the way to resolving the problem and look forward to 'returning home', challenges can still appear.

9. Leading to a 'twist in the tale' that might be a final hurdle. But the end is in sight –
10. And the hero resolves the problem, which is the object of his / her quest and so restores balance and harmony to the world.

Elaborating on these much-simpfied ideas could take up a book in itself. But you can see how the basic structure of story fits with the desire to shape ourselves and be the author of our own lives. Above and beyond introducing these ideas to the children, you might ask the following sorts of questions…

- Pick a story you really like. Thinking about the ideas above, why do you think that story has made such a powerful impression on you?
- What does 'noble' mean? What kind of noble qualities do you think a hero has?
- A villain does not have to be a person, but might be an idea or a feeling inside of us. What feelings could we say are 'villains' in people's lives?
- The villain is the opposite of the hero, and shows 'mean' qualities or characteristics. What different meanings can 'mean' have? What can a villain's mean qualities be?
- Based on stories you know, why do you think the partner-character is important? How can a partner help the main character? If you were the hero in a story, what would your partner be like?

See also Chapter 6 Developing Resourcefulness for more on the links between narrative, metaphor and boosting emotional intelligence.

13

Values – the ruler inside us

Values, as the name suggests, are fundamental principles that are important to us; they tend to inform our actions and provide a measure against which we can assess our interactions with the world around us. If we are to raise children's self-awareness and so develop their emotional intelligence, then this is an important area to address.

Knowing more about their values can help them:

- motivate themselves when things seem difficult. By linking potential beneficial outcomes to their values something with which they are struggling can become a worthwhile challenge. Encourage them to ask themselves, 'What makes this classwork/ activity/conversation "necessary" to me?' How will this help me? Which of my values does it support, or how can I adjust my view to make it relevant to my values?
- become more aware of what makes them happy (or otherwise). When an activity aligns with a key value happiness or contentment is often the outcome. An awareness of this can assist with making choices in life. Conversely, of course, the root of some deep-seated unhappiness can be when actions and values are misaligned. Simon has encountered this several times when coaching individuals who are unhappy with their current life situation. For example, consider the effects on someone who values helping others, yet has drifted into a job s/he has come to believe exploits people.
- understand why they choose to behave the way they do in different situations. Why do some colleagues appear brusque in meetings and on training days, yet are caring professionals who go the extra mile in the classroom and staffroom? Why do some children behave as they do for you, yet not for other colleagues? What is it that these individuals value?

The most obvious way to elicit values is to ask, 'What's important to you?' This general question will yield a range of answers, some equally as general, some specific. Try it on yourself first. Aim to come up with at least ten answers. Can any of these be merged? Are there any patterns? Look for the Big Idea behind the more specific answers (e.g. 'It's important to me that I play squash at least once every week,' might reveal a value of keeping fit and healthy). This straightforward activity alone is a useful thinking task and can produce some revelatory introspection.

Some example values that could be used as prompts:

Being a good son/daughter
Honesty

Respecting others
Friendship
Fairness
Working hard
Understanding others
Living healthily
Helping others
Earning lots of money
Competitiveness

What others could be added to the list? Discuss whether a value could ever be something negative, or if there is likely to be a positive side to any value.

Other activities connected to eliciting individual values include:

- Life Purpose. Ask the children to describe to each other what they believe their purpose in life to be. If they were sent here for a reason, what was that reason?
- Yearbook. Tell them that you would like to write a yearbook that includes every member of the class. What values would they expect you to mention?
- The Shape of My Values. Ask the children to order their values from the most important to the least. Will theirs be list-like, a line from the most valuable value downwards, or will it be pyramid-shaped with one value at the top, then two equal second places and three equal third? Which values, if any, do they find difficult to rank one above the other and why?
- Value-Based Decisions. Provide a scenario for which individuals must choose a course of action. The scenario needs to allow for more than one course of action (see website for some ideas). The class can then divide themselves into groups (or place themselves on a continuum, depending on the scenario) and discuss their reasoning. Different-answer groups can be formed to debate their reasons and related values, or same-answer groups can get together to discuss their key value in making this decision and look at other values they hold to see where other similarities and differences are. Useful questions for tasks include: What did you base your decision on? How have your values affected your decision? What might have helped you arrive at a different decision? Provide another scenario and see if / how groups divide this time.

As suggested earlier, we also subconsciously assess other people based on our values; we see if they 'measure up' to what we expect our friends or colleagues should be like. If we value being charitable, it is unlikely that our best friend will be selfish. At this point, it is important to be clear that values and behaviours are different. Values are principles that guide us; behaviours are actions. So, it is possible that a quiet person may have a loud friend (they may both value social interaction, but behave in different ways when demonstrating it). In the case of our charitable values example, these may be revealed by the behaviour of giving money or time to the less fortunate, whereas a selfish person would be behaving out of line with his / her values by demonstrating this behaviour and, should we know this, then we would interpret the actions as having an ulterior motive. And this is where we need to be cautious. We can't see values, but we can see behaviours.

Sometimes we might 'get a feeling' about people one way or the other, but often it's through constant exposure to others' behaviours that we start to understand the values by which they live.

You can clarify the difference and learn how much the class know each other with the following activities:

- Return to the earlier list of values (including any that were added by the children), or their own list of values. Ask them to describe some behaviours that might reveal each value in everyday life. What would the person be doing? What would they expect to see? Prompt by asking them to clarify how a 'good' son / daughter might behave, for example.
- Ask the children individually to think about a friend, then ask them to list what it is about this person that they like. Which are behaviours and which are perceived values? Do the behaviours support the identified values or suggest other values?
- Tell the children that they will be invisible for one day so that they can secretly observe someone with whom they would like to be friends. What values would they hope this friend would have and how would they be able to spot them?
- Ask them to think about someone from history who they admire, a well-known person they look up to, or their ideal job. What values do they believe this person has or this job requires? What might this reveal about the children and their values?
- Ask them to think about being a nurse, a stockbroker, a teacher, or even a knight and / or any career of your choice. What values would you expect someone from each of those professions to have? Suggest they compare their thoughts with others in the class to see if there is a consensus. Extend by asking them to write a person specification for each profession that includes their expected values (see Table 13.1).
- Challenge one of the values of the above professions by suggesting a scenario where the person behaves in a way that seems to contradict the agreed values for that profession. What reasoning can the children come up with for the behaviour? For example, it might be agreed that the stockbroker values earning a lot of money, but works for free in a homeless shelter in the evenings.
- How much do they know about each other? The children should write down their values, already revealed through an activity, making sure their name is on the top of the paper and place them in a bag you have. You then randomly select some of the lists. From the values you read out, the class have to work out which class member is being described.

Because getting along with other people is desirable – and an emotionally intelligent thing to do – it is important to respect others' values. This does not necessarily mean we have to agree with them. An important maxim in coaching is that the coach is never critical of the coachee. This is especially true of their values, the foundation of the person. It is easy to imagine the detrimental effect this would have on the relationship and any progress that both parties had hoped would emerge from it. It is a thought worth sharing with the potentially emotionally intelligent coaches in your class.

How will respecting the values of others be beneficial for both parties?

Table 13.1 Values – knight's

Knight of the Realm	
Candidates for the above position must have at least the following:	
Values	Bravery Nobility Chivalry Honour
Qualifications	A noble title (Misters need not apply) Horse riding (level 2 or above) Weapons training – minimum of sword, lance and mace (level 4 or above) Fairytale creatures – capture, taming, slaying
Experience	Jousting tournaments Distressed damsel rescue (from bone-crunching ogres, wicked stepmothers, fire-breathing dragons, or evil curses. Everyday distresses not admissible, e.g. stubbed toe)
Knowledge and Skills	As well as the above, the candidate needs to demonstrate knowledge of: Battlefield strategy Wall scaling Table manners Courtly dancing

14

Belief – what we think we know

One of the guiding principles of this book is encouraging children to think. Emotional intelligence is about being attuned to self and others, something that involves heightening our awareness of us in our surroundings and how we interact with those sharing the space, reflecting on this, considering options, imagining what effect a particular action might have, and so on. In other words, *thinking* in various forms. Beliefs, however, are about *accepting* in-formation we have encountered as true and generalising this to the world around us ('everybody has a cruel streak'), as well as to 'how we are' ('I'm shy') and 'how we might perform' in different situations ('I'm no good at exams'). On the whole, there is little thinking involved in belief. So how are they formed?

Ask your children this question (delete as required):

'What are English / Irish / Scottish / Welsh / American / French people like?'

We have no doubt that there will be a large number of generalisations (it was, after all, inviting such answers), though racist comments are unacceptable as always. Follow up these brief answers with another question:

'Where did you get those ideas from?'

This is the most interesting part, as the children delve around for when they first formed their notions. Incidentally, anyone who answered the first question by saying that all Welsh people (for example) are different from each other should give themselves a pat on the back.

Here are the sorts of things you might hear:

I saw one on TV (note the dehumanisation).
My dad used to work with a _____ man once. He said he…
Wasn't it a _____woman who…?
We see them on holiday.
They eat…
They dress…

Experiences that shape belief may be firsthand or secondhand; if a child meets a person from another culture s/he may generalise from that, or they may accept the judgement of another who has met the person. In the same way that we need to be aware of how our own interpretations can sometimes be skewed, accepting another's experience uncritically is to allow someone else to make decisions on our behalf.

To raise awareness of this, try these activities with your class, follow any with a discussion of how we can sometimes leave others to shape our beliefs for us:

- Newspaper Stand. Examine a relevant but contentious newspaper story as told from the perspective of two 'opposing' newspapers. Look at them separately first, asking the children what the writer's opinion is and how they know this. When comparing the two, look at the difference in descriptions, language, information used. Whose opinion is right? What makes them think that?
- New Stand. The activity could be extended by asking them to rewrite either story from a third paper's perspective or that of a person in the article, or by asking them to describe a newspaper's likely view on a range of other matters, and / or by noting down examples of words and phrases each newspaper might use when writing about another well-known issue or person.
- Photo Story. Put up a range of photos from newspapers around the classroom. What might the caption read? If using people not known by the class, ask them to describe the person in the photo: what they are like as a person, their likes and dislikes, even the type of film they like, food they eat! Do they think they could be friends? Why / why not?
- Quote Appeal. Select excerpts of quotes from books, newspapers and the Internet. Present them without explanation of the content or person. What do the children think about this person? Why?

We are of the opinion that people usually form beliefs in one of two ways: (1) at some watershed moment in their lives, or (2) through constant exposure to the same or a similar source.

1. Watershed moments – this is when something happens to the individual that is a defining moment in their lives. Imagine the impact that a visiting American teacher would have in a small primary school where few of the parents can afford holidays, let alone take their children to the US. This might be the first or only opportunity some of the children have had to meet an American citizen. Every aspect of that visitor's appearance and behaviour is likely to be scrutinized, and it is likely that s/he will become a reference point whenever Americans are mentioned thereafter.

As the term 'watershed' suggests, such out-of-the-ordinary experiences will usually be linked to strong emotions. We may easily recall the death of Princess Diana or JFK because the shock of these events makes these memories more easily and more likely to be remembered than most. Events that have a strong emotion attached to them are encoded and retrieved differently from other types of memory. Ask the children which events stick in their memories and why they think this is.

2. Constant exposure to the same or a similar source – this might be firsthand (if that American teacher mentioned above is around every day, for example, then the outcomes from that original watershed moment are reinforced), or secondhand (from a friend, parent, the family's newspaper, etc. telling us their views).

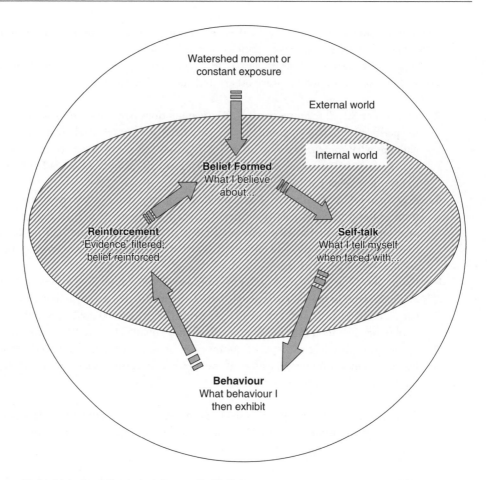

Figure 14.1 Formation and reinforcement of beliefs

Let's look at the other stages:

- Belief Formed. This is now our touchstone for future dealings with this issue. Unless critical thinking is applied, every encounter (whether an observer would judge it positive or negative) is likely to reinforce this belief.
- Self-Talk. We are reminded of our views on the issue through internal chatter reasserting previous 'evidence' we have gathered on the subject.
- Behaviour. This reflects our expectations in an encounter with the issue. Our responses are primed in readiness and the outcomes from these will be visible for all to witness.
- Reinforcement. We select in-formation from our latest encounter to support our belief and ignore anything that contradicts it, therefore reinforcing our previous view.

If people believe that teenagers are unpleasant, then that is what they will perceive. Evidence to the contrary, if noticed, will be dismissed as an exception. This is the filtering referred to on page 53.

With this cycle of belief we can see how the lines of opinion and reality can become blurred. Furthermore, because it is only our behaviour that is visible to others, *their* beliefs about us might be formed at this stage. Our beliefs can influence reality. Ask the children to consider this scenario:

There is a group of people / a new boy or girl in your class you do not like because of your beliefs about them.

1. How do you behave towards them?
2. How do they respond to that behaviour?
3. How do their responses reinforce your belief?
4. What do others not involved in this exchange see you doing?
5. What belief about you might they form after witnessing this behaviour?

Unhelpful beliefs can be challenged at any stage of the cycle above (see Overcoming Obstacles page 71). The real skill is in individuals recognising a belief in themselves and then having the courage to challenge it, as the results may change their view of the world. Beliefs can be comfortable ideas to hide behind; the world can be polarized, for example, making opinions and choices more clear cut. At a personal level, beliefs can help avoid challenge and formulate excuses.

Below are some other links to belief formation and some activities to raise awareness:

■ Stereotypes. Beliefs about 'another group' to our own distinguishes between 'us' and 'them', whether we are thinking of ourselves in terms of socioeconomic class, ethnicity, culture, religion, and so on. Anything that perpetuates division between people cannot be considered a good thing. Many of the activities above can be used to question these beliefs.

■ Templates. This short-cut way of thinking does have its uses in many everyday activities. Using 'templates' can simplify the world and move things along quicker, rather than always having to examine the features of every new thing we encounter:

    ■ Family Tree. Take an everyday object and draw it into its family tree. So, a shoe is a type of footwear that is an item of clothing. What other branches will come out from the footwear and clothing stages? How much further do the branches subdivide? What about links to clothing from other cultures? Examples from flora and fauna (the top of two major family trees) work well in this activity as well.

    ■ Bring in a photo of an everyday object from another culture or period of history. Ask groups to work out what it is and how they reach their decision. Discuss how they used categorisation skills to identify to which 'family' the object belonged.

    ■ Creature Feature. What makes a dog a dog? How do we recognise one as such and not as a cat? What are the features of each of these main categories? Ask the children to identify a group of animals and write a description of them for their friends to work out.

■ The drawing board. Are the templates above the best they can be? Use any category of animal (or other groups you have looked at) and ask for them to be redesigned to be the best they can be for their environment (or purpose).

15

Overcoming obstacles (or belief 2)

Ask yourself one of the following questions (you might choose to ask similar ones of the children):

- What skill would I really like to acquire?
- What burning ambition do I have?

Follow this up with:

- What has stopped you from doing this so far?

The answer you give to this question may well be a limiting belief. Write the answer down and read it yourself. Is it really true? When did you decide that this was the case? How did you reach that decision? Does it look like an excuse?

Beliefs can encourage or inhibit movement towards goals and are often at the heart of coaching experiences. It follows, then, that in order to coach themselves or others towards a more emotionally intelligent way of living, the children need firstly to be aware of beliefs (see page 56). Second, they will need to know how to challenge the unhelpful ones when they arise. We have used Figure 14.1 on 68 to structure some activities to raise awareness and suggest challenges followed by a grid to provide some suggestions of practical approaches to coaching self.

1. Formation stages

Challenging unhelpful beliefs before they become embedded is obviously the most desirable point at which to address such issues. We can divide beliefs into two categories: those we hold about ourselves and those we hold about others. We will deal with both.

All human beings are essentially the same creatures with similar needs. Without getting embroiled in the nature-nurture debate here, it is possible to accept that our different environments will have an impact on us. However, we share a number of similarities that could form the foundation for us all viewing each other equally, whilst acknowledging our individuality.

- Similarities and Differences. This adaptable activity provides ways of showing how several items can have a difference and still sit comfortably as members of the same group. Provide lists of objects for the children and suggest that these have a range of similarities and differences (e.g. car, train, ferry, tank, truck, fighter aircraft, van). Their task is to name the whole group and list what they all have in common (e.g. vehicles: used for carrying things, all have engines, etc.). Next, they can categorise the objects; there might be five in one group and two in another (e.g. fighter aircraft and tank, both for warfare); pick one out that is different from the others (e.g. ferry), explain why and then do it again with another object (e.g. train); use a Venn diagram to highlight what certain objects have in common with each other that are different from others. When they have tried this activity you might choose to give them the name of a group for which they have to come up with a number of items (e.g. you ask for 3D objects and they write down cylinder, sphere, etc.). Besides demonstrating their ability to identify the similarities and differences and categorise accordingly, it is the articulation of their thinking, their metacognition, that is important with these activities. Transferring their learning to the human experience can be aided by the following activity.

- Categories in Common. Ask the children to give themselves a category name into which they all fit (e.g. Year 5, Class 7RH). How might they divide themselves into subgroups (colour of eyes or shoes, hairstyles, etc.)? Ask them to move into those groupings and then form themselves into other groups. Children should see them-selves and others moving around groups of different sizes and with different members. What does this tell them? What does reforming into a single group let them know? What have they learnt?

- The People's Foundation. Place the class in groups, the more diverse backgrounds for each grouping the better. Ask them to write down as many ideas as possible for what all people have in common. Suggest that you are looking for similarities that you cannot see (rather than physical ones). Start them off with all people needing shelter and wanting to be happy. During the process you could ask them to define their ideas further, like what it is or what it takes for someone to be happy. Alternatively, you could have a member from each group visit other groups and provoke thinking by constructively questioning what they have written. Form a class consensus and make a 'foundation stone' with their ideas on. Display this in class.

Negative *self-belief* can be addressed in similar ways.

- Cross Purpose. Everyone writes down the end of this sentence: 'I am good at…' Encourage them to think broadly – activities, subject areas, (inter)personal skills – and make the point that you only want them to think of *one* of the many things they are good at. Alongside the completed sentence they should now write what it is that makes them good at it (e.g. concentration). They should list as many reasons as pos-sible and in as much detail as they can. Now share with a partner. Next, they complete the sentence, 'I would like to be better at…' and are then asked, 'What from the first part of the activity can help you achieve this?' Notice the presupposition that some-thing will be found.

2. Self-talk

Simon has a friend with what some might consider an unusual kind of persecution complex. This friend, a highly respected professional, once told Simon that traffic lights 'always turn to red' when they see him coming. Let's be clear: he was suggesting that these mechanised signals had singled him out and then communicated with one another to plot against him! A ridiculous notion when reframed in such a way, but what he was noticing, his 'filter', would trigger internal chatter every time it happened ('Look, they're doing it again! I don't believe it – every time I come down this road…!'), which would progressively embed the belief a little further. You could liken this to when children believe that they are not 'sporty', 'musical', 'mathematical' or 'arty'. Focus in on the issue by questioning them sensitively until you reach what they have been telling themselves that has been generalised to the whole activity / subject area: I can't hit a ball, we can't play musical instruments in my family, I can't do fractions, I can't draw. Now the belief can be challenged.

- Reframing. Rigid language can fix attitudes, so it is useful to be aware of the sorts of words and phrases that can produce such mindsets (or set minds). Persuade the individual to re-evaluate using some of the ideas below. Questions will usually revolve around getting to the truth (often not consciously acknowledged until asked), defining the specific issue and planning a way towards improvement.
  - Can't, e.g. I can't hit a ball. Is this something that they are finding unable to do at the moment? Should 'yet' be tagged on to the end of the statement? Or are they being non-specific and need to improve a skill related to hitting the ball (e.g. harder, straighter, more often). Or is it simply being unwilling to do it – *won't* rather than *can't*?
  - Never, e.g. I never get invited to parties. Is this true, or is it that they want to be invited to more parties? What was the last party they went to?
  - Always, e.g. they are always noisy. When weren't they? What happened?
  - Must or should (+/– not), e.g. I should be quiet until I'm spoken to. Suggests the voice of another who has helped the individual internalise the belief. We like to challenge 'rules' if there is no basis for them, however these should be approached with caution. A question might be, 'What might happen if you did / didn't?'
  - They say that…(and similar), e.g. They say that sparing the rod will ruin the child. An obvious question follows this: who says? One of the most prolific ways that opinion is passed off as truth in conversation. Always worth a challenge (especially such daft assertions).

For more about language use we recommend *Introducing Neuro-Linguistic Programming* by Joseph O'Connor and John Seymour.

It can be too easy to talk ourselves into 'failure'. In his *Inner Game of Work* book, Timothy Gallwey introduces us to Self 1 and Self 2. Essentially, Self 1 is the bossy and judgmental voice which impedes our performance, whether through reminding us of our previous setbacks or through barking distracting orders at us ('Get ready, she's about to shout "go"! Don't trip up again! Remember to push away hard at the start!"). The other self, Self 2, is the embodiment of 'inherent potential', which athletes and musicians experience when 'in the zone'.

- Hearing Impediments? Use the following (or similar) to examine Gallwey's thoughts on inherent potential and the effect of negative self-talk on it. The object is to help the children realise what they can do 'naturally' (e.g. roll a ball) and to notice any self-doubt and how it manifests itself. Suggest they notice what they are doing and what they are saying to themselves whilst they wait for their turn and during the event. Allow everyone to have at least two goes at their group's activity. After their second attempt ask them to consider how confident they felt between turns and what was going through their heads. How much did these thoughts help or hinder?
  - Can Bash. Like at the fairground, set up a pile of cans to be knocked over by a thrown object.
  - Skittles. Rolling a ball to knock down skittles. How many can they do?
  - Pile 'em high. Stacking items in turn to see who can put the most on before it collapses.
  - Tower of Blocks. Taking interlocking blocks from a freestanding tower. Who can take the most before it falls over?
  - Sculpture. Provide a picture of a model for the children to replicate in clay.

- Who's there? Ask the children to notice the 'voice' next time a limiting belief arises.
  - What does it say? What words are used when talking about 'not being able to' do something? Write these down and reframe (see above).
  - Whose voice is it? Where did it come from? What was that person hoping to do (e.g. help the child improve at a sport, or protect him / her from something potentially dangerous?). They probably meant well. The children should imagine that person sitting quietly now, watching and smiling, allowing them to find their own way. No matter what happens, the individual will see that the child is doing his /her best and is pleased by the progress being made.

3. Behaviour

Have you ever avoided talking to someone because you thought they looked grumpy? They could be quite amicable and are unaware of the unfortunate impression they give. Perhaps they would love to make more friends, but are shy. Or a lack of confidence has caused them to adopt a defensive demeanor...or maybe they really are just grumpy. But why? Simple activity: smile and say hello. Ask how they are. How do they respond?

- Trying out Behaviours. To adjust this activity for the children, you might ask them to think of a teacher who they believe is 'always telling us off' (notice the language of belief). What behaviour in themselves might they change to break the cycle? Or they could think of someone in the school who spends break time on their own. It might not be because they want to be alone. What would happen if they were invited to join in and were treated as a friend? Where else could the children try different behaviours and observe their impact? In an argument with a friend? When being reprimanded by a parent? When threatened by a bully?

- Observing Others' Behaviour. The children could choose to observe how a friend behaves when communicating with others in a range of situations. It is useful to note the facts of the interaction as well as their own thoughts on what is happening. For example, one entry might read: 'Katie was asking a favour of her mum. She looked at her the whole time, used "please" a lot and began jumping up and down to make her point. She seemed desperate and her mum eventually gave in. Perhaps Katie knows this way of asking will help her get her own way with her mum. I don't think she would like Anna to see her doing this, as Katie is much more forceful and confident with her.' After a week or so, the observer could write a perspective of the person. How might that compare with the subject's internal world? Does the observer think that the subject would agree with the suppositions being drawn? Turning it around, what judgements might others make about them based solely on their behaviour? Do they think that any adjustments to their behaviour would be warranted to reveal the 'real' person?

Sometimes beliefs are formalised into superstitions. Often, such beliefs can serve a practical purpose in affecting the behaviour of those who believe such things. Whether superstitions came about in such a mindful way is open to discussion. However, when we present the well-known one of it being 'unlucky to walk under ladders', we can see that this could have been crafted as a warning (especially if someone is painting up there).

- Superstitious Behaviour. Collect together some superstitions and explain that these are forms of belief. Suggest that someone may have invented them, but to do what? Ask the children to suggest a reason behind each. They could be in the form of say-ings (as above), or as folklore. Here's a selection of both to start you off:
  - Lucky to throw a coin into a fountain
  - Lucky to leave a house through the door you entered
  - Lucky for a bride to wear something borrowed
  - Lucky at New Year to have a dark-haired man come into your house before any other visitor, carrying coal, salt, bread or money (neither Steve nor Simon meet the criteria for this anymore)
  - Lucky to buy a car from a rich person
  - Unlucky to break a mirror
  - Unlucky to step on a crack on the pavement
  - Unlucky to cut a loaf of bread at both ends
  - Unlucky to put a calendar up before the new year
  - Unlucky to pass people on the stairs
  - Ginny or Jenny Greenteeth. This creature lives in water, her habitat recognis-able by the green weed on the water's surface.
    - Rusalki. Another water-dwelling creature, found mainly in rivers. They emerge at night and lure unsuspecting victims into the water to live with them.
- Extend this activity by asking the children to make up their own. They might begin with a behaviour that they want to encourage or discourage and then devise a saying or a creature to bring it about.

4. Evidence

Let us return to perception is projection (53) – a fearful person will see danger all around him / her; an adventurous person will live in a place that is wondrous. This is their 'map of reality', their perception of the same physical world, and their filters will ensure that new evidence supports this view. Now imagine a young white boy from a financially poor background who is struggling in class and bewildered by school in general. The news one evening announces that most white working class boys do not do well at school. He hears this and concludes that school is not going to make him feel valued because a group to which he knows he belongs 'fails'. It is confirmation that his feelings were right. The difference between what the report said and what he heard is not relevant anymore, what is relevant is what he does next. Give up? Put his efforts into something in which he thinks he will be valued? Or work harder to contradict the statistics? Without the understanding and support of those around him, it is possible that he will become part of a self-fulfilling prophecy. Henry Ford once said, 'Whether you think you can or think you can't, you're right'. His words are often quoted, but that does not diminish their power.

■ Number Crunching. Take a look at statistics and what lies behind them. Does *some* mean *all*? If 53 per cent of parents think that sugar is bad for children, what do the other 47 per cent think (we just made that figure up, but if we hadn't how would that affect our perception of sugar or mothers or children?)? If four out of five girls have low self-esteem (sorry, more made-up figures), what about the one in that five? What helped her have a better view of herself? How can these lessons be transferred? To our mind, this is about (1) turning the figures around to find out what that tells us, (2) thinking about how figures affect our perceptions of the issue under discussion, (3) figures being unjustly linked to a cause (e.g. if it were true that 99 per cent of prison inmates didn't study law, is that really related to them being incarcerated?), and (4) the accuracy of the figures. Many activities can come out of these four points. For example, in *Countdown to Non-fiction Writing* Steve cites the 'number-glass' idea of seeing figures both from a half-empty and half-full perspective. These alternative statements about the same scenario illustrate the point: less than 200 people bothered to go to the meeting / over 180 people flocked to the meeting. While the numbers are similar, the way they are framed strongly influences our reaction.

Table 15.1 Dealing with limiting beliefs

	Identify by...	Challenge by...	Resolve to...
Formation of belief	Examining your thoughts and feelings when encountering new experiences.	Questioning the belief that is forming. Examples: • 'Poor' performance in an activity. What did I need to do to do better in the activity? How can I achieve this? Was there anything happening around me that affected how well I did? • Negative view of a person. What might have caused him/her to behave like that? What do I already know about this person that does not support my experience? • Negative labeling of a group (racial/cultural / socioeconomic / etc.) based on the behaviour of one / a few. How similarly might a different group behave in this situation? What word would I use to describe the behaviour of this individual/group and how could I experience the opposite in other members of the group elsewhere?	Make a list of ideas for improving my performance next time and practise. Change anything in the surroundings that I am able to. Talk to that person in a different situation. Find out more about them next time. Treat other members of the same group you meet for the first time as an individual independent of that group. Avoid 'pre-judging' (prejudice)
Self-talk	Listening to what the inner-voice is saying, at the time or later, about the experience.	Questioning in-formation (as in the Formation stage), and re-framing rigid language (see above) that can fix attitudes. Examples: 'The teacher *never* picks me. I *can't* play sport. I *always* get the answer wrong. I'm *no good* at working in groups.	Be open to possibility and be wary of language that closes off these routes.

Table 15.1 Cont'd

	Identify by...	Challenge by...	Resolve to...
Behaviour	Noticing (1) when your behaviour towards others is 'out of character' with how you see yourself, or (2) when you feel stopped by a feeling from doing something that others can do.	(1) Using 'new eyes'. Stop, smile (if appropriate) and treat *now* as the beginning of your contact with this person. Notice them for the 'first time' and be open to what they are saying. (2) 'Becoming' another person to overcome behaviours brought about by personally limiting beliefs. Imagine that you not only can do this activity, but that you are the best in the world at it. 'Try on' the attitude of that person. And, again, start from now.	Be the person you want to be. Write a list of adjectives that describe this person, or think of a person who you would like to be more like and write down words and phrases that describe them. Plan how you might realise these descriptions.
Reinforcement	Watching out for just as I expected' thoughts, being eager to confirm label and stopping paying attention (or simply giving up) during an encounter.	(1) Noticing your 'filters' in action. Ask yourself: what did I ignore in that encounter? What evidence was there that did not support my previous opinion? (2) Ridiculing your belief. Write down the negative belief you are tempted to reinforce and then write down ten reasons why it is silly to think that.	Assume that people's intentions are good (similar to the Principle of Purposefulness see Chapter 5) and that they are similar to you – progressing through life, wanting to be happy, seeking to be valued . . . and occasionally misunderstanding others and making mistakes.

16

The winged football and other metaphors

We've already touched on the idea of metaphors – for example the Simile Game on page 5 and Ride a Giant Butterfly on page 32. In this section we want to emphasise both the power and pervasiveness of metaphors in our language and the fact that they exert subtle but powerful influences on our perceptions and the way we think.

By way of illustrating this, Steve recalls that during a school visit the children were questioning him about writing and being an author. At one point the teacher asked 'And as an author, how do you deal with writer's block? What do you do when you hit that barrier?' Perhaps you've already spotted the two dangerous metaphors that she used (and the suggestion of inevitability in the word 'when')? Steve said, 'Well, I put a doorway in it and walk straight through'. Then, looking at the class, he said, 'Or we could...?' And the children responded with –

- Use a trampoline to jump over it.
- Turn into the Hulk and smash through it.
- Hire a hot air balloon and sail over it.
- Strap on a jet-pack and zoom over it.
- Be a mountain climber and clamber over it.
- Turn it into smoke so it blows away.

Afterwards, Steve mentioned to the teacher that if she habitually called the phenomenon of not having the right words available 'writer's block' and regarded it as a 'barrier' that's how the children would perceive it.[1] It would come to feel very different if it were called a writer's opportunity, a writer's playground, a writer's rollercoaster ride – or any number of more positive and more helpful metaphors.

The very fact that metaphors 'run in the background' of our language and thinking can make them insidious. Steve has a real issue (which perhaps Simon will coach him through) with metaphors commonly used in education. We have 'targets', learning 'goals', 'objectives' 'league' tables and 'cohorts'; 'programmes' are 'in place' and we 'cover ground', although while some children manage to 'keep up' others 'fall behind' or 'slip back' because learning is such an 'uphill struggle' – in which case they need to be 'pushed' or 'stretched' (but surely not at the same time) and, most cruelly, 'drilled'. This is the language of sport and competition or, more darkly, of the military; a cohort for example is a Division of the Roman army. Interestingly, and ironically, while these ugly metaphors are used quite freely with children, the influence of political correctness puts pressure on some people to invent increasingly obscure and supposedly inoffensive terms in certain cases. Steve recently worked with a bottom–set class who, he was told, had to be referred to as 'the Quest group', though the kids themselves were quite open about the fact that they were in Set 5. The good intentions behind the optimistic terminology were noted, however.

One danger of metaphors like these being used unreflectively is that they subliminally communicate assumptions which 'colour' people's perceptions. We might not be aware of them and yet can be affected by them. In this case the whole concept of learning becomes tinged with the idea that it *is* competitive and *will be* difficult – though of course children are more likely to succeed if they are 'risk takers' and 'move beyond their comfort zone' while 'thinking outside the box'.

Activity

You can of course point out to children the metaphors that are currently embedded in the language of education. But whether you do or not you can ask the class to imagine that learning, for instance, were an orchestra or a playground or a garden and, having planted that seed, see what results grow out of the activity to help the children flourish.

Combining positive and helpful metaphors with the 'as if principle' can have dramatic effects. Steve worked with Ben, aged nine, who suffered from very low self-confidence. He said that he felt safest in his back garden at home. Steve suggested that they could make up a story together using that idea. 'So once upon a time there was a cosy back garden... Do you want to be in it?' Ben said he did. 'And you were there when suddenly –'

'There was a shadow'. Steve asked about the shadow. 'Oh, it's because of the high wall', Ben said. 'But there isn't really a high wall around my garden', he added. 'It doesn't matter', Steve told him, 'we're in the world of make-believe now so it's only pretend'. After a brief discussion Ben wrote the following tale.

'And Ben was in his garden playing football. Only it wasn't much like football because there was nobody else there to play! So Ben had been kicking the ball against the high wall. But this was getting boring, so he tried to see if he could kick the ball right over the wall. Well, he kicked and kicked but the wall was too high and the ball kept bouncing back to Ben's feet'.

'Then he had an idea. Because the garden was a magic place, Ben put out a wish and the ball suddenly grew wings! Then, when he kicked the ball it sailed right over the wall very easily. Ben decided to imagine what it would be like to *be* the football. And so he did and went sailing over the wall. It felt great! The End'.

'Is it the end', Steve wondered, 'or do you maybe want to add something to make that story even better?' Ben considered this and shook his head. 'No I'm happy with that. The football can fly and have lots of adventures, but he can always come back to the garden whenever he wants to'.

You may have noticed perhaps how Ben referred to the ball as *he* just then. The symbolism of the story is obvious of course but writing it made Ben feel good. It also had a positive effect on the boy's self-confidence, so his teacher reported later. Subsequently Steve couldn't help thinking that Ben had no trouble committing his thoughts to paper whilst remaining within his comfort zone.

Creating 'metaphor stories' can be useful in helping children (and adults) to deal with issues and limiting beliefs in an elegant and effective way. Ben may not even have realised he was addressing his confidence problem, especially since the notion of a winged football doesn't belong to the 'real' world – though it does significantly belong to the world of 'making beliefs'. Furthermore, the symbolic energy of such stories operates subconsciously (often more so than at a conscious level) where our 'map of reality' is lodged. Thus any changes prompted by stories of this kind tend to be deep rooted and occur automatically, without the conscious effort of trying to behave in that way.

Having said that, one can work with personally meaningful metaphors in a cognitive way. Steve remembers a hypnotherapy client, a highly creative man named Alan, who was having trouble starting a number of writing and illustrating projects. He found himself in the strange situation of really looking forward to doing them, but felt nervous and reluctant whenever he intended to get going.

In the course of his hypnotherapy Alan recalled as a child often being shouted at by his mother. She was, he said, very overwrought and going through some difficult circumstances. 'So I learned not to argue. In the end I just tried not to draw attention to myself'. Following close on the heels of these memories came the recognition[2] that his present anxiety was about *not wanting to draw attention to himself*, something that would surely happen if his books were successful. That was the 'linking theme' of those early childhood incidents and his current predicament.

During the relaxation phase of the hypnotherapy sessions, Alan had reported some 'bizarre imagery' drifting through his mind. He thought first of a dark place and then realised it was deep under the ocean, a sterile area. Then he saw undersea volcanoes, glowing lava, cascades of bubbles and the water shimmering with heat. He decided that these images represented both his suppressed anger at not being able to express himself and also his 'creative energy wanting to burst forth but not being able to'. He felt that the sheer weight of the ocean meant that the volcanoes would never be seen, and that there was an endless futile struggle between the water and the fire.

In talking this through with Alan, Steve mentioned that scientists had discovered such 'deep sea smokers' as Alan had described were havens of life in an otherwise dead region. 'The warm water is rich in minerals and each smoker is a miniature ecosystem'. This prompted Alan to apply further rationales that helped him to see the imagery in a different way. He realised[3] that the water had a 'calming effect' that prevented possibly cataclysmic eruptions of the volcanoes. The ocean allowed the heat of the lava to dissipate gently and, as Steve had suggested, in a life-giving way. Alan also decided that when writing a book it's not helpful to have 'one big burst' of creative energy, but that a gentler and more sustained inspiration is far more productive. 'And all of those bubbles are like ideas and good feelings rising to the surface', he suggested shortly before the end of the session – admitting that he felt much better about himself ('effervescent' is how he described it) and raring to start on the book he'd been putting off.

So with all of this said, how might we make use of the ideas in the classroom? Here are some suggestions –

- Help children to notice the way metaphors are embedded in the language. Show them how to 'catch themselves on' as and when they apply unhelpful and negative metaphors to themselves. A light and playful approach often helps in this. A child once told Steve 'I can't write a story because I'm thick'. Steve said 'Well pretend you're thin for a while and show me when you've finished it'. The child laughed at that, went away and carried out the task (see also the Triangle of Failure on page 31).

- Encourage children to play with metaphors, so finding fresher, more positive and more useful ways of representing ideas.

- Build 'metaphor play' into your EI work with the class. If the feeling in focus is anger for example, ask how it would feel different if it turned into a kitten or a ladybird or a winged football.

- Display inspirational posters – better still, encourage children to design their own; some highly effective results can be achieved by matching a suitable picture with an appropriate quote, both readily available on the Internet. (A word of warning however – check for cynicism. Steve noticed a classroom poster that said 'Shoot for the moon. At least if you miss you'll fall among the stars' – to which one prematurely jaded ten-year-old said 'No you won't, you'll re-enter the Earth's atmosphere and burn up'!)

- Help children to see that myths, legends, hero tales, parables etc. can be read as allegories of today's real-life problems. Speculate about what the golden fleece could represent, or Medusa, or the Argo. In this case what modern day enterprises might Jason's adventures parallel?

- Encourage 'therapeutic story-making'. A good way is to have children retell traditional fairy tales. A slightly more challenging activity is to combine the motifs (defining features) from different fairy tales to create new stories. One way of launching this is to mix and match story titles, for example 'Cinderella and the Three Bears' or 'Snow White and the Golden Goose'. (You'll be pleased to know that Steve did this activity with the Quest group and they made a great job of it!)

17

Managing emotions

Tomorrow is the day it begins. Everyone has been on tenterhooks for weeks and now the school has had the phone call. You lay in bed, wondering how your interview will go. You imagine them coming into your lesson, watching what you do, listening to what you say, noting how the children respond. Your palms are clammy now. You feel sweat trickle down your back. You can actually hear your heart and wonder if your partner will be woken by its juddering through the bedsprings…

We all know the impact that an imminent visit from Ofsted can have on many teachers – and we apologise for inducing that horror for some of you now – but it makes the point that our thoughts can influence how we feel, both physically and emotionally.

Being able to manage emotions is another aspect of being emotionally intelligent. 'Managing' is not bottling up, finding a place and time to vent, or becoming the ice king or queen; it is about keeping emotions from clouding your thinking. Approaching a situation in a resourceful manner is one such way of doing this. In the example above, knowing that you are well-prepared, having anticipated the questions you are likely to be asked and now just needing to have a good night's sleep to be fresh for the inspection is an example of viewing a potentially challenging situation resourcefully. Any areas for improvement raised will provide a continuation point for your professional development. Simon has coached many middle and senior leaders in education and, when an Ofsted visit was imminent, this was the way the vast majority chose to respond.

This was how they 'chose to respond'. We use the term deliberately. In his multi-million selling book, *The 7 Habits of Highly Effective People* (see Bibliography), Stephen Covey recounted the story of Viktor Frankl, a Jewish psychiatrist imprisoned in the Nazi death camps. Though tortured and abused, Frankl came to realise that he retained the 'last of the human freedoms' – he could choose how to respond to his treatment at the hands of his captors. He later reported that he used his imagination to 'see' himself lecturing his students back at home, commenting on what he was learning from his imprisonment. It is a grim story, but one we find inspirational; in the most adverse conditions one person realised that he had a choice of how to respond to what he was subjected.

Where there appears to be no choice, we can still choose our response to the situation. Happily, however, we often have more freedom in that we can choose not to put ourselves in unpleasant situations again.

- Charting Highs and Lows (1). Ask the children to keep a 'diary' for a week, one where they make a note of their mood and what might have caused it. Provide some graph paper where they should write key times across the bottom axis (e.g. 9:00 am, midday, 3:00 pm, etc.) and a scale of 1to10 up the side axis (1 = very low, 10 = very high). At key times in the day, they should rate their mood between one and ten (a discussion in class at the beginning of the activity would be beneficial in helping them assess what a three is, for example). Next to their rating, they could add more information, including a brief description of their feelings, what might have contributed to that rating, or what they were doing at that precise moment.

- Charting Highs and Lows (2). Instead of having set times to report, the entries could be more random, perhaps when they are feeling a particularly distinguishable mood, doing a specific activity or just when they feel like it.

The activities above might feed into a class compilation chart, be the basis for further research around the school or, most importantly, open up discussion on how emotions might be managed more resourcefully by the children.

- Discuss some of the extremes of emotion, such as joy, anger and sadness. Ask what other people might notice about them and what they notice about themselves when they feel each of these emotions. They might be surprised at how differently from others they act. Raising awareness of others' mood indicators may be helpful in smoothing communication, handling misunderstandings and nurturing a more supportive class environment.
- Discuss some of the situations that make them sad, angry or scared. How would they like to react? What would need to happen for them to be able to do this? Work on issues in small groups to formulate action plans (you might want to refer to Chapter 25 for how to create one of these'). Obviously, this is an area that needs to be handled with sensitivity and care.

Sometimes we make decisions or do things that we later regret. As is the enduring message in this book, learning from such episodes is crucial; however, does this help us in coming to terms with what might be haunting episodes? You might like to use this:

- Note regret for no regrets. Leave this with the children for their own time if there are any decisions they have made or something they have done that they regret. They should begin by writing down the regretful situation and then answer the following questions:
  - What do they regret about it?
  - What can they learn from it?
  - How is it hindering them now?
  - Is there anything they can and want to do that will make amends?
- If yes to the last question, plan out what they want to do to 'make things better'; if not, memorise the learning point and ceremonially shred the paper on which they have been writing! These final acts should be seen as an end to any turmoil caused; its metaphorical destruction.

Bizarrely, whilst we were writing this section, Simon was rung by Ofsted who wanted to speak to his wife! All reacted calmly and there were no sleepless nights.

18

El and the three-legged stool

The activities we have provided so far can help you nurture emotionally intelligent dispositions in the children. These also provide the underpinning for developing young 'creative coaches' who, with practice, can help others become more positive and resourceful in their life journeys. One of the most rewarding aspects of being a coach is that you are constantly learning from other people. And with such practice and learning, the skill to self-coach becomes ever more a reality. So, let us look at how, specifically, we can help the children start coaching.

Picture a three-legged stool – you might even see a milkmaid from yesteryear sat upon it. Take away any one of the legs and there is no support for the other two (nor for anything resting upon them); they are interdependent. The three-legged stool is how we visualise the three fundamental skills of coaching: building rapport, asking questions and listening carefully to the answers. Of course there are other skills a coach should have, however without these three the sessions would not get off the ground.

■ Android interviews self-promoter. Ask the children to pair up and decide on a famous person who they would like to interview. They (or you) decide who will be the interviewer and who will be the celebrity. The former then writes down five questions that s/he would like to ask the celebrity (without revealing them yet), whilst the celebrity thinks about what information s/he would like to communicate in the interview (e.g. something about their latest album, a film they appear in, moving abroad, their car collection, etc.). When the interview begins, the interviewer must only ask the questions already written and the celebrity must answer them, but should also take every opportunity to say what they want to say (the new album, etc.). At the end of the interview, ask the pairs to think about how much listening was going on, what they noticed about the questioning (and answering) and, if this was real life, how well the two individuals would have got along. They might want to think about any televised interviews they have seen and, under the three headings of Q&As, listening and relationship, what have they noticed that has made a successful interview? Rules for running a successful interview could be developed from this and practice ones trialed.

We have all probably cringed at the inattentive interviewer and the blatant self-promoter in such situations. This activity should help the children realise how the three basic skills provide a firm foundation for interviews and other modes of (mainly) spoken communication. In the following sections, we will look at how to develop these skills, not for interviews, but for the far more profound discussion that takes place between coach and coachee.

19

Effective questioning (first leg of three)

Most children say their first words around the age of one. Soon after they begin stringing those words together several months later, they start asking questions. Between the ages of two and three, the questions seem to become endless (we can imagine those wan smiles of recognition on parents' faces now). There is real skill and a purpose in these unconsciously formed questions. What we would like to do here is to raise awareness of these questions and then develop that skill to enable question selection for effective coaching practice.

- Different questions, different answers. Write up the following questions for the class to see:
  - What is 2 + 2?
  - What is the capital city of England?
  - Do you like orange juice?
  - 'Are you tall?
  - What is green?
  - What is your favourite film?
  - How far away are the stars?
  - Why do we have best friends?
  - How can we find true happiness?

Ask the children to discuss what they notice about these questions. They might even try answering them and comparing their answers; what do they notice then? Ask about the meanings of some of the words in the questions, for example what is 'tall', a 'friend' and how might 'happiness' differ from 'true happiness'? And what about the purpose of some of the questions? Is it useful to know how far away all the stars are (and is it possible to answer?), or is there a better question we could ask with a more specific purpose? Play around with the questions, add your own – get them thinking!

This is a useful way of opening up a dialogue about questions and questioning. Some points that we hope the children would realise include:

a. Different types of question produce different types of responses;
b. Questions are useful even if there is not one absolute right answer;

c. Suppositions and opinions are sometimes perfectly good 'right answers';
d. Questions can be worded precisely or in a 'fuzzy' way – and both can be useful.

Let us reinforce these ideas with some more activities:

- Question hunt. Ask the children to find:
    - Some answers that are always right for everybody;
    - At least one right answer that is different now from what it used to be (for example, Pluto used to be called a planet but now it's known as a dwarf planet);
    - A couple of questions where different people's opinions can be counted as 'right' answers;
    - A question that nobody really knows the answer to;
    - A question that makes you and your friends want to ask lots of other questions (for example, 'Is it better to be alive now than it was a hundred years ago?').
- Questioning the answer. How many questions and types of question can be found for these answers?
    - Mount Everest
    - Onomatopoeia (Simon has always liked this word – ah-ha, a first question!)
    - 12
    - String

When it comes to asking questions in coaching, there are straightforward rules (though not to be confused with 'easy in practice'): questions should be short, simple and should stimulate thinking. Short questions allow clarity of thought for the coachee. Keeping the question simple, by using uncomplicated words or phrasing and by avoiding multiple questions in one utterance, allows the coachee to focus on the issue rather than translation. Thinking is stimulated through allowing the coachee to talk, explain, describe, clarify, justify, consider, analyse, evaluate, and all the 'thinking in words' that is done in the course of a conversation. The difference with coaching is that the coach does not get in the way of this process, merely prods and prompts it; a coach will not do what most people do: try to 'help' by giving possible solutions. Suggesting answers disempowers and, at best, only offers a short-term solution for the individual. The long-term intention of coaching is to empower individuals and to bring about independent, solution-focused thinking. The main question-type with which coaches do this is the 'open' question.

Quick quiz – how many of the questions at the beginning of this section are open questions? Many people's definition of an open question is one that begins with one of the five Ws (Who, What, Where, When, Why) or How. If you are familiar with that definition, you may have said that there were seven open questions. But that would have been incorrect. Ask yourself how many capitals of England there are or how many answers there are to 2+2 and you will see that these are not as open as the definition suggests. Closed questions are often defined as those to which only a 'yes' or a 'no' can be answered; to this we would add anything that yields only one answer, as do the two examples above. So, there are actually only five open questions at the beginning of this section.

- Name the celebrity. This game should bring home the value of an open question in arriving at a resolution. Everyone is given a famous person's name. They should not tell anyone who it is. In small groups, individuals will take turns at asking one person questions about their celebrity. The questions must be phrased so only a yes/no answer can be given and the answers must not be misleading. The object is to find out the person's name in the least number of closed questions. A guess ("Is it...?") counts as a question. When half the members of each group have been questioned, find out the different number of attempts it took and any strategies used by the class to get to the answer. Explain the difference between a closed and open question and then ask them to continue with the game, but this time asking only open questions. Repeat the debrief at the end and find out whether the open or closed questions worked better. And if they have not figured it out already, you can tell them the most useful open question to ask here – 'who is your celebrity?'

Schools can be precise. The necessity to transfer curriculum knowledge often dictates that there is a right answer and a wrong answer to what the children write and say. To use Bloom's (1956) terminology, this is at the bottom of the cognitive domain's taxonomy; it is a feat of memory and no understanding is required (e.g. what is the capital city of England?), no real thinking is needed in relation to the 'answer'. Despite increasing numbers of teachers seeing the benefit of teaching at higher levels of Bloom's taxonomy (which will also aid memory), testing of the knowledge is still mainly a memory test. But there are some issues that are discussed in school that often *need* to work at a higher thinking level.

- Open questions open up thinking. First explain what an open question is (if you have not already done so) and then ask the children to work in pairs with the issues below or similar. They should take turns at asking the other open questions about a selected issue, avoiding asking any closed questions or offering advice; just open questions that their partner answers in role. They then swap roles, choose another issue and begin again.
  - You want to join in with a group of kids, but daren't ask.
  - You want to eat more healthy food at home, but your parents keep giving you ready-made meals.
  - You want to be elected to the school council.
  - Your room is always untidy. You would prefer it tidier, but can't be bothered.
  - You want to stop over at a friend's house, but your parents don't like him / her.

(Some example questions might be: What is it your parents don't like about your friend? What have they said? Who have they spoken to? How might they have formed this opinion? How have you tried to persuade them so far?)

The above task will probably be more challenging for the children than it first seems. There would have been a temptation to offer advice – explicitly or implicitly. Notice any closed questions into which individuals may slip. An analysis of these may reveal one of the main outcomes of using closed questions in coaching – advice in disguise ('have you tried...?') or in deep, deep super-spy disguise, by closing off options with a solution waiting nearby ('do you sometimes...?'). You could ask the class to share any closed questions that slipped out and then encourage some metacognition by asking them what was going through their mind when they asked the question. Were they trying to figure out a solution for their partner by any chance? Easily done at this stage.

The activity could also be quickly revisited using a useful coaching statement in place of open questions. This, again, opens up the thinking as the description, analysis, evaluation, etc. unfolds. For the questioner, it opens out the inner world and allows them to choose an area that might yield more thinking for the talker and so move them towards their own resolution. The statement? "Tell me…" – Tell me more about that / them / the situation / the people involved.

Having said all that, there is a place for closed questions in coaching. Mainly it can be used for clarifying and checking to ensure understanding of what has already been said, or rhetorically for reflecting back something of interest that the coach picked up on so that the coachee can consider its significance ('did you notice that you just used the phrase…?'). See also the use of closed questioning in the Coin Flip Game (page 49). However you might find the use of closed questions would be confusing at this early stage, so you may want to leave this out for now.

20

Really listening
(second leg of three)

You're in the staffroom. You're talking to a colleague. You want to tell them about a breakthrough you've made with a difficult child with whom they are also familiar, but as soon as you mention the name the colleague interrupts, expecting tales of more problems and setbacks and regales you with their experiences (once again) with the child in question. Sometimes, they may identify a possible solution, 'You know, it would help if s/he would listen more!'

Mis(sed)understandings, mis(sed)communication, frustrations on both sides and inappropriate actions taken in response to these can all result from poor listening. There are several reasons why this might happen:

- Distractions (internal preoccupation or external occurrences);
- Expectations (of topic and/or speaker);
- Associations (with keywords or topic);
- Benevolence (wanting to provide a 'solution', some allegorical advice, or helping the speaker find the 'right' word(s) to express him/herself);
- Expedience (looking to fulfil own agenda or steering the speaker's conversation to make a point of their own).

'Listening' could be arranged on a scale from the more physical 'hearing' (perhaps accompanied by the hearer making some polite acknowledgement noises for the sake of social graces) to variations of the more cognitive 'listening'. How (well) people attend to a speaker's utterances has often been categorised and presented as 'levels of listening' (e.g. Whitworth *et. al.* (1998), van Slyke (1999), Thomas and Smith (2004)), where the attention of the listener moves on a continuum from themselves to the speaker and their message. The levels on such a scale have been much debated, but, in our opinion, these are less important than having the self-awareness of knowing whether you are listening absolutely to the speaker or not.

The ideal-listener end of the continuum is that to which coaches aspire. Obviously listening to what is being said is crucial, but so is being aware of how the message is presented. In practice, this includes considering the content of the message, hearing the words used, tuning into any significant language patterns (such as repeated metaphors), noting the tone, checking against paralinguistic cues of the speaker (like body language) and being receptive to what is not being said. This is quite a list for anyone; however, it can be summed up as *really* listening. And sometimes the thought processes that coachees go through in explaining their issue to a good listener in an open and supportive environment may be enough for them to reach a resolution in how to proceed.

The positive effects of someone really listening to us can be profound. Does it make us feel special? That we have something of interest to say? And how has that affected our views of that person? Warm? Compassionate? How does being a good listener in the classroom (and staffroom) affect the relationship you have with your children (and colleagues)?

Conversely, what negative impact does a distracted listener have on our esteem and on the disclosures we then choose to make. If it happens several times with the same person, we may form a judgement of that person as 'not a good listener' and someone we might not open up to with more personal issues, or if we receive the same treatment from several others in a short space of time, might we decide that there is something wrong with how we communicate? People's unwillingness to listen can be a cause of conflict on an interpersonal level, as well as on an intergroup and international scale.

- Noticing Listening in Others. Ask the children to notice examples from everyday life (in class, when they go shopping, when they play, on the television, etc.) where people are not really listening to others. How do they know they are not listening? What would they need to do to improve? What do the children think would happen if they really listened? Make notes and report back.

It's a busy life for many of us and there seems little time to pause and listen. Here is a simple, worthwhile (in)activity to raise some awareness of what surrounds us.

- Just listen. Ask the children to do exactly this. What do they notice when they listen now? Ask them to write down all the things they have heard. What has surprised them?

Something they might have noticed is the running commentary inside their own heads. We first encountered this chatterbox in Chapter 14 (see page 68). It has a comment for most things: what we do, say, think, experience, who we meet. Sometimes it has useful things to say; other times it can be a nuisance. What were the children's chatterboxes saying during this activity?

- Recording the Chatterbox. The children could start to notice the commentary of the voice in their heads during activities and, most usefully here, during conversations. What is the voice saying? What is its tone? What feelings is it producing? A more structured version of this activity is 'Hearing Impediments?' in Chapter 15 (page 74).
- Speaking, Listening, Thinking. Ask the children to listen to a friend who will describe a holiday or hobby to them. The listener concentrates on what is being said and notices their own thoughts, but must say nothing. After the monologue has finished, they share what they were thinking and feeling throughout the description. Finally, ask them to draw a storyboard together of some of the key moments in the conversation and to add their thoughts in bubbles.

Different cultures have used storytelling for millennia to capture the history and traditions of their people. Less grandly, when someone asks us how our day went or what we did at the weekend, we are likely to launch into a short story or to share an anecdote of a particular event; nobody responds to the question by listing facts (if they did, they probably would not be asked that – or any other – question again). It is likely that the questioner could recount the story for a third person. This prolific storytelling default suggests that the human brain is hardwired to tell and to remember stories.

- Telling Tales. Arrange the class into small teams of equal number and ask them to number themselves one, two, three, etc. Whilst the others are busy with another task, you tell all the number ones a tale of appropriate length. The number ones must then tell the twos without the rest of the team hearing; the twos tell the threes in the same way and so on until all have heard the tale from the previous team member. The last person in each team must then retell the tale to the original storyteller. Where were the mistakes (if any)? At what point(s) in the chain did the story go wrong?[1] What happened to make it go wrong? What might be done to communicate a more accurate tale next time?
- Instruction (to) Manual. Another activity for checking listening is to give step-by-step instructions orally to the class. This could be used for simple tasks, like preparing to do some writing, or more complex activities that involve working as a team. It can also be used in any area of the curriculum (e.g. for baking a cake, using new computer software, etc), but ensure that all words that will be used are already known (e.g. icon) to cut down on other-than-listening interference.
- Emphasising the Point. Build up listening and oracy skills by getting the children to practise saying some phrases with the emphasis on different words in the sentence. Start them off with a short example, like 'I am a good listener', stressing a different word in turn each time and asking for an interpretation (possible explanations in this case, respectively, could be: *I* am, not *you*; yes, I really *am*; *one*, not more; rather than an *inattentive* listener; rather than speaker or writer). Give each pair two cards, one each, with a phrase on with which to practise.

The above activity is especially useful for raising awareness of how judgement may be accidentally conveyed in a conversation (e.g. 'what did you *do*'?). To maintain an open and trusting relationship between coach and coachee, it is important that the coach does not express judgement in any manner (see Chapter 21 on rapport). For this reason, it is also best to substitute the question-word 'why' with 'what'. You can see what might happen:

- Why did you say that to him?
- What was the reason for saying that to him?

Because 'why' is often associated with criticism, the first question might be seen in that way; the second is less personal, with the focus shifted onto the reasoning. It may be worthwhile practising rephrasing 'why' questions as 'what'.

- First listen. This activity is for any time one person wants to talk through something with another. It is best for them to first try it on a close friend who wants to share a problem, as they will really want a good listener. Advice to listener:
  - Stop what you are doing and look at your friend's eyes when they are speaking.
  - Listen carefully to what they are saying (as if you might be tested on it!)
  - Nod and agree at the right places.
  - Ask open questions about what they are saying, but don't interrupt.
  - Show you understand what they are saying by sometimes using sentences like, 'So, you mean that (and repeat what they said).'

What did you notice (when you did the above) about:
- What your friend said and did?
- What the chatterbox inside your head was doing?

21

Building rapport
(third leg of three)

Next time you walk into the staffroom take a careful look around at the people there. How are they interacting? You will probably spot the pair in easy conversation, you may see someone on the edge of their seat, annoyed about something (what is the listener doing?), and is there a huddle in the corner? Is anyone looking disinterested, distracted or displeased? Do people look like they are enjoying each other's company?

How do you know all this? Reading body language is one of the main ways of identifying if people are in rapport or not. Rapport – derived from the Latin *portare* meaning 'to carry' – is about communicating or connecting harmoniously with others, messages being 'carried' with ease between individuals, people getting along together. It is essential for this harmony to exist between coach and coachee if any 'opening up' and progress is to be made. It is also, of course, an emotionally intelligent behaviour.

■ Observing Rapport. A good introductory activity to this topic that will raise awareness (and questions) for the children is to look for rapport around them. Once you have explained what rapport is, ask them to find examples of it in the world. There may be examples to record during a weekend activity, something on television, or at school break time. As examples are gathered, they need to write down how they know that rapport is taking place. You might also want to point out that they don't necessarily need to be listening to the conversation either.

There is scope with this activity in that they could also be asked to find the opposite, people not getting along (soaps will be a good source). The class could be divided in two, one half as 'in rapport' seekers, the other half for 'out of rapport'. The feedback will yield a range of ideas that should be unpacked for further consideration. Perhaps they would want to devise a list of instructions for an alien visitor.

Basically, we know when we are *in* rapport with someone and when we are not. It is an unconscious realisation that, when made conscious, can help someone *build* rapport and make the other person feel more at ease in conversation. This can lead to more fruitful and open discussions.

■ Matching. Coaches have been known to use this technique to quickly bring about rapport and maintain it. It involves *approximately* reflecting the other person's body language.

It should not be an exact replication or the other person will feel they are being mocked. Try this out by having one speaker telling another about their weekend, hobby or some subject that will produce sustained talking. The listener should match the speaker's body position by placing themselves in similar positions, so one arm on the desk can be copied, as can an approximation of how they place their legs. However, they must not follow every little move, like scratching their nose. The listener should just know that they are going to talk at length to someone with whom they do not normally work. Afterwards, ask them how it went, what were their thoughts and feelings whilst speaking? Then tell them what was happening.

A variation on the above could be to prime some of the listeners to break rapport (mismatch their body language, look away, etc.) at an agreed signal. What does the speaker notice and do? What did they think and feel?

Body language is more than just the movement of limbs. The most basic of ways to start building rapport with others is to smile. It is a good way too, as smiling is uplifting and infectious. Eye contact whilst speaking to someone helps maintain rapport, letting them know that you are interested in what they have to say. Facial expressions, showing sympathy at an appropriate moment for example, can also harmonise communication. For more on this area we would recommend the work of Paul Ekman, the psychologist who proved the universality of facial expressions and who is the most prominent researcher in the field of reading people's expressions (www.paulekman.com).

- Caption Competition. Quiz the children on their reading of body language (and on their wit) by asking them to put words to pictures. Photos from magazines and newspapers are useful sources.

There are other clues that let a speaker know when we are in rapport, both non-verbal and verbal. Listening carefully means that you are able to ask pertinent questions and make the right noises at the right time, allowing more possibility of rapport taking place. However, signals that we are already in rapport once again include those normally unconscious indicators, such as matching the tone, volume and speed at which somebody is speaking.

It is possible to raise awareness of an area we could call 'voice rapport'. Again, this is not about mimicking the coachee, but showing awareness of how they are feeling by not addressing them in a tone of voice that would be counterproductive for the mood they are communicating (e.g. a jovial sounding coach for a coachee communicating sadness). Reading emotion through voice is a useful skill to practise to become more emotionally intelligent.

- A Change of Tone. Practise saying an innocuous phrase in different ways. For example, try 'Good morning!' in a 'bright and breezy manner' (think holiday camps of the 1950s), then in a dull way, then abruptly, next in a bored manner, etc. When your repertoire is ready, use it on the different children as they enter the classroom. On your board have already written up, 'How is Mr/Mrs/Miss_____ feeling today?' Discuss findings and then ask them to try a range of tones with different phrases.

Rapport is natural. It is interesting that we can feel someone is 'on our wavelength' by how they respond to us even if we are not consciously aware of what the responses are. Raising awareness of these abilities allows us to practise the skills to build rapport quickly and maintain it. As with many things in life, it is all about successful communication.

Building rapport is just one leg in the crucial skills tripartite of coaching. Next we need to look at how we might bring these three together to move a coachee forward.

22

A coaching model

Many coaches like using models of coaching as a way of structuring the process and of ensuring that the coachee moves towards a resolution in a resourceful manner. Often these models are acronyms that suggest movement either upwards or onwards and encapsulate good coaching practice. We would like to offer an alternative approach to achieving the same, something that provides structure, yet latitude for individual coaching creativity; something that can be applied basically or with more complexity to provide an even more powerful development process; something that allows the coach to work flexibly with their new learning.

Our approach brings coaching back to just two questions that sum up what it is setting out to do. These questions are 'What do you want?' and 'How will you get there?' As a backdrop to any coaching conversation, these two questions keep the focus on formulating a goal (question one) and on the process of achieving it (question two). A third question, 'How did it go?' can be used at a later stage to review the whole experience; if it did not go as expected, then what was positive about what did happen and what did we learn when things did not go as well? If necessary, how might we approach this differently next time? What would we do again?

- Target Practice. The most familiar of areas in which to practise these three questions at this early stage will be with the targets you set for the children to achieve. This will be applicable to any subject area in the curriculum, whether in KS2 or KS3, and you might choose first to model the process in your one-to-one target reviews with them over the preceding lessons. In their practice with peers, begin by writing up the three questions and then pairing up the children to work through them. Let them know that it is okay to ask other questions within each of these areas (open questions are best here) if they think it will help their partner have a better idea of how s/he will achieve the target. Tell them that, by the end of the conversation, you want both parties to have a very clear idea of what actual things the respondent will do, the steps they will take to ensure they achieve this target. Below are examples of the course that conversations may take within each of the question areas:
  - 'What do you want?' – this is self-explanatory, as they will probably just read out one of the targets you have set for them. It could be anything: remembering to start sentences with a capital letter, using more primary sources in their work, planning their work before starting and so on.

- 'How will you get there?' – this may be met with a response of 'I don't know' or simply a reframing of the target (e.g. 'I'll plan my work before starting it'). This is where the questioner will have to prompt some deeper thinking through challenges. Encourage them to be creative, but be ready with prompts like 'What might Jack or Gill do to reach this target?' (when they say they don't know), or 'How will you do that then?' and 'What's stopped you from doing it already?' when they are giving an imprecise answer. They might find that a large part of achieving this target is simply remembering to do it. In this case, the questioner could ask 'What might help you remember to do this?' Other questions might focus on a technique they might use for the target, such as in the 'planning-work-before-starting' example above. To be successful at this, the questioner needs to accept that there is no right or wrong way of doing it, to be creative and flexible with the questions they ask because they are following on from the answer their partner provides, and that 'all' they need to do is to help the other person find a way that works for them of achieving that target.
- 'How did it go?' – this stage obviously follows a little later, perhaps in a week or so. The question itself should elicit a lot of feedback that could take the respondent into the realms of metacognition (thinking about their thinking) as they provide more detail. The more confident questioners might want to ask about what worked particularly well and what didn't (followed by what might be done to improve the outcomes next time).

This first practice will help the children see that they already possess the basics of what is needed to move their friends on successfully. The skills will further develop over time with practice, but even at this early stage there is the likelihood of some creative questioning and use of language to urge their peers to look at issues from a variety of perspectives. Even now, as suggested above, interesting insights could arise from the stimulation of metacognitive processes that will benefit the learner into the future.

In the following sections we will outline in more detail the components available beneath each of the questions. We will help the children to select thoughtfully which of these to use, based on their growing awareness of how best they can help others and of where their own strengths lie. This framework brings together the emotionally intelligent attitudes and coaching skills promoted in this book. It will help both the coach and coachee become more self-aware, that foundation stone of emotional intelligence, and hopefully improve their view of their lives and of the lives of those around them.

CHAPTER

23

Appreciate now

Before we embark on a journey of positive change with the children, it is important for us to highlight the positivity in our present. We do not believe in change for change's sake, yet even when people want to make alterations or strive for something more to enrich their lives we believe that it is worth them taking some time to appreciate what they already have. We are sure that, like us, you have heard some people bemoaning their 'bad luck'. 'That's just typical of my luck!' seems to be the stock phrase (have you ever heard anyone use that phrase when talking about something positive that has happened in their lives?). How many of these people have their health, their family, a good job, a comfortable house, food and water, holidays, laughter, friendship or all of these? It is extremely unusual to encounter someone who does not have at least one or two.

The act of simply stopping and appreciating now can be an energising and uplifting experience. It is something worth doing before striving for new goals. Who knows, the reconnection might reveal in the present what they thought they needed from the future? Below are some suggestions on how you can supplement this appreciative experience for the children.

- Counting Blessings. With your children, have the discussion from our opening paragraph above. What do they have to be thankful for? Ask them to make a list or to tell a friend. You could focus on personal qualities, in which case their partner should tell them which qualities they are thankful their friend has and why.
- Box of Gems. Suggest they keep cards, gift tags, letters, e-mails and messages from people who have demonstrated appreciation for them in some way. For verbal comments, recommend a notebook and keep everything together in a box. Delve into it to remind themselves of how much they are appreciated, or to lift the spirits.
- Personal SWOT (strengths, weaknesses, opportunities, threats). This popular business and coaching tool can be introduced as a way of appreciating now and linking this to the future. Every child should divide a sheet of paper into quadrants, labelling each with one of the words. The first two are self-explanatory. Opportunities are positive possibilities that they see for themselves at this moment in time, and threats can be seen as the more negative possibilities looming. A discussion with a friend could centre around how their strengths might assist them in dealing with the threats and in developing their opportunities, and how their actions might lessen their weaknesses. In this way they take stock of what they already have at their disposal. How could the friend add to their partner's perspective of him/herself and the issues as they see them?

- The Bank of Thanks. It is good to know you are appreciated. The children in your class will know this – ask them how they feel when you compliment them on a piece of work or thank them for their help in running an errand. Write up the words they use to describe these feelings. Would they like to help others feel like that? When they appreciate their present situation and understand the positive roles played by those around them, they might feel that they want to 'pay back' some of this kindness. They could:
    - Offer to do a job for that person;
    - Make and send them a 'thank you' card, explaining exactly what they are thanking them for;
    - Make them a gift, perhaps within a relevant lesson.

- Wonder Wall. This is a fun and enlightening activity that can be used for a number of awareness-raising purposes. Provide every child with a sticky notelet on which they will write the answer to your question. Depending on the area in which you would like to raise their awareness, the question might be:
    - What is unique about you?
    - What is your best quality?
    - What is the best thing about your life?
    - What positive words would your Mum / Dad / carer use to describe you?
    - What have you done that other people may find interesting?
    - What might surprise your classmates about you?
    - How have you helped someone?

Ask different tables to stick these up in different areas of the room and then have everyone circling to read each other's. If you have asked the children to write their names on the notelets, you might encourage individuals to select one (not their own) about which they know more information and can explain to others.

- Wonder Wall (Now and Later). You might want to turn this into a wider activity that appreciates now and also prompts them to think about themselves in the future. In this case, use two colours of notelet to denote the two times. Future-based questions could include:
    - What would you like to do when you are older (not necessarily career-based)?
    - Who would you most like to be like and why?
    - What country would you like to visit and why?

- Take a wander around. This is great for adults who lead busy lives, but also for children who, as they grow older, may be starting to lose that sense of wonder about the world around them. Going for a walk and looking afresh at nature, for example, is a great way of reconnecting with now. Quieten the children and ask them open questions to help them notice what is going on around them. Lay on the ground and look at the grass (smell it and touch it too); watch an insect making its way through this 'jungle'; lay on your back now and watch the clouds drift or hurry; notice the wind making the leaves dance; run your hands across the bark of a tree. Take a wander around an urban landscape too or the school grounds.

Quick questions to appreciate now:

What is good about now?

What in your life makes you smile?

What do others like about you?

To whom would you most like to say 'thank you'?

What makes you glad to know parent / carer / friend?

What do you like about your local area?

Figure 23.1 Quick questions to appreciate now

24

What do you want?

'What do you want?' Ask everyone in the class that question and you are likely to get a whole range of answers. Like many open questions it is vague enough to allow the respondent's interpretation to fill in the lack of clarity. The objective is the same, though: 'what, that you do not have here and now, would you like to have'? A favourite toy from home, a best friend, a television, a career in television, a sibling, money, some sweets, superpowers… Not everything is coachable, nor do some things require coaching. If the solution to an issue lies outside of that individual's control, or if there is a problem that requires clinical or specialist intervention, then coaching would be inappropriate. However, when coaching is required, we need to ensure that the conversation balances vagueness with laser-precision clarity in order to first elicit and then focus in on clear-cut, achievable goals.

Goal setting is an effective means of starting a new journey when change is required. As with literal journeys, reasons for travelling vary from person to person; some want to leave a certain problem behind, others want to experience something new. Whichever is the driving force, the process of change is framed positively for coaching. So, whether an individual states that s/he wants to stop getting poor grades, for example, or whether it is improved grades that are required, the coach should always help the individual adjust the focus towards a more positive potential achievement, as in the second example.

- More Reframing. On page 73 we looked at reframing to overcome obstacles. Ask the class to reframe the negatively stated goals below, so that there is a more positive focus each time. Add any more you feel are appropriate.
  - I don't want poor grades any more.
  - I want to stop arguing with my friends all the time.
  - I don't want to eat unhealthy food any more.
  - I don't want to be on my own at breaktime.
  - I don't have time to do my homework.
  - I don't want to be unhappy at school.

Also key in setting a goal to work towards is precision. You may have noticed that even when reframed into a positive, there can still be a vagueness about the goal. It is in the wording of the goal that absolute clarity needs to be achieved. The more tangible it is, the more fully the coachee will be able to experience the goal in the present, priming both the conscious and the subconscious for what is to come. The result is that the coachee can 'buy in' more to their goal and so be more motivated to achieve it.

- Precision Reframe. Using the example of the positive reframe 'I want to improve my grades', ask the children what questions might elicit a more precise goal. Questions that clarify aspects of the statement are a good start: 'What do you mean by "improve"?' might receive an answer relating to specific grades. Suggest they adjust their 'More Reframing' answers to provide precise goals to work towards. What questions might they have asked a coachee for each one?
- Precise Slice. Divide the class into groups and provide each with a few sentences that have a word cut from them and replaced by a more non descript one (some examples are below). Their task is to experiment with a variety of words to see how these alter the sentence without changing the meaning. Can they explain the differences (or even nuances)?
  - The play was *interesting* (e.g. funny, hilarious, amusing, inspiring, thoughtful, thought provoking, intelligent).
  - She was *tall*.
  - *Good* children get to choose a dessert.
  - He *hit* the ball all over the court.

Add more challenge and thought by slicing out two or three words from longer sentences.

- Synonym Sidestep. One child (A) has to help another (B) find out what word A has in front of him / her. Any explanation may be used by A, though s/he must not use synonyms (e.g. for clues for the word 'stack', A must not use 'pile', 'heap' or 'mound'). A variation on this game is not allowing A to speak at all, only to mime or draw. Turn this into a team game and have one cardholder and three guessers in competition with another team. Those who work out the most words win.

One way to enable a coachee to make their goal more tangible, to heighten what has already been brought about by eliciting a more precise goal, is by asking some sensory questions appropriate to the goal, such as:

- What would that look like?
- What would you see?
- What would that sound like?
- What would you hear?
- What would you feel?

Listen to the answers the coachees give to such questions. Sometimes they are stated in the present tense, as if they are actually there already.

- Being There. Ask the children to close their eyes and listen carefully to every word you are about to say. Take them on an imaginary journey involving all the senses. Take them to the sea, a lake, into the mountains, a forest – you decide. What can they see? Pause. What do they hear? Pause. Smell? Feel (inside or through their skin)? Afterwards, they could describe the place to a friend and explain what they were experiencing.

They could also compare their experiences and write about them. How powerful were their imaginings?

Merely setting a goal can help motivate an individual to move forward; however; such questions and activities as outlined above can reinforce the 'buy in' to a particular outcome and make the individual more resolute. Questions such as 'how will that help?' assist in perceiving the goal from a slightly different angle and prompt what are effectively justifications from the coachee; reasons to achieve that they re-cognise, hear and acknowledge themselves. Again, that attachment to a goal is reinforced.

- Drawing out Goals. Sketching out (and colouring, if desired) what effect the goal will have can help to fix the coachee on where they want to be and so set them off on their journey with the end in mind.
- Stepping-Stones. This tool urges the coachee to assess how close they are to the place they want to be. It is also useful in helping them evaluate aspects of their lives to find an area in which they want to work. Imagine the centre of the diagram as an island surrounded by water with stepping stones across it to the mainland. To use the tool, each child labels the six paths with an area of their life (e.g. family, friends, school, etc.), or with parts of one of those areas (George, Julie, Jordan, Rajesh, etc.) and decides how far along the path they are – from the centre outwards – towards where they would ideally want to be, represented by the outer border. They then colour in how far they have reached. So, on a path labelled 'school' they might colour the first

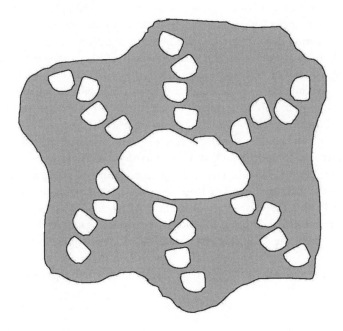

Figure 24.1 Stepping stones

three stones of the path because they are broadly happy with the situation there, but there are some smaller issues they would like to improve. From here, the children can share their completed Stepping Stones diagram with a friend who will coach them on one of those areas for improvement, remembering to set precise goals. Other follow up activities could include small group discussions and writing exercises. The latter could be extended writing about the positives, or on templates stating, for example, the pros and cons that led them to colour in a set number of stones.

Bringing all the above ideas together into a fluid coaching conversation obviously takes practice. However, the basics at this stage are to:

- Elicit a positive and precise goal
- Encourage the coachee to really 'buy in' to their own goal

Example coaching conversation (Part One)

Below is an example of how a coaching conversation might begin. This is only one possible sequence, drawing on the elements mentioned above. Not all may be necessary, nor may this be all the stages, as questions are guided somewhat by what the coachee says.

- Dissecting a Coaching Conversation. There are a few things to notice in this example. Why not copy it and ask the class what they notice about it? Pair them up, perhaps, and suggest they read it aloud in role.

Most noticeable in this conversation is how the mood of the coachee seems to lift the more she describes her goal. This seems to be in part due to the sensory question and also to the question that asks for 'great' to be translated. Notice that the coach kept the question short, so as not to interrupt the flow and yet heighten it at the same time. Earlier, honing the goal brought some clarity to the description – for both coach and coachee – whilst the same clarity was brought to the final, agreed goal when the coach restated it for both to hear. This demonstrates for the coachee that she is being listened to and, tacitly, reaffirms for both the positivity of the experience.

In conclusion to this section, goal setting should be realistic, rather than fanciful. The children need to understand that their aspirations should be achievable, but that does not mean that anyone should quash challenging goals. In fact, challenge can be a motivator as long as the goals are clear. Any large goals will mean moving through a series of smaller ones first. With the sense of achievement that each smaller success brings, individuals can be reinvigorated and, to use the journey metaphor again, can have time to take in the scenery, check their compass and reassess their ultimate goal in view of their experience to date.

In the next section we will be dealing with the practical steps towards those destinations.

Table 24.1 Coaching conversation 1

Coach	Coachee
What do you want?	Not to be sad when I'm at school.
Okay, so what is it you *want*?	To be happy at school.
What does 'happy' mean to you?	Smiling and laughing, feeling like everybody is your friend.
So, what would it be like to be happy at school?	I would enjoy lessons and work with different friends; breaktime would be full of games and fun.
When you think about that, what do you see, hear and feel?	I see lots of smiles. And the sun is shining. I can hear lots of chatter in the classroom, excited but not silly so the teacher doesn't tell us off. There would be laughing and singing at break. It feels great!
What is 'great' like?	Like I'm filled with sunshine!
So, what you want is to be happy at school, to see all these smiling faces around you, hear the sound of fun and laughter and to feel great, like you're filled with sunshine?	That's it!

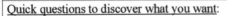

Quick questions to discover what you want:

What do you want to achieve?

What would that be like?

How will that help?

What exactly does XYZ mean to you?

How will that look / sound / feel?

What will you see / hear / feel?

How will you know when you've done it?

Figure 24.2 QQ to discover what you want

25

How will you get there?

A training day somewhere on the other side of the country. Simon drives, Steve takes the train. Our reasons for travel are the same, it may be the same distance from our homes, yet we choose different modes of transport. Both of us have legitimate reasons for our choices, making our journeys quite different. Neither is right nor wrong.

This metaphor sums up coaching and the importance of choosing our own paths (or means of travel) because of what works for us, rather than someone telling us that they have always cycled to that destination and that we should do the same. Coaching respects the unique knowledge of the individual and helps release his/her resourcefulness in order to generate and make choices and then take actions that will move them towards their goal.

■ Same Destination, Different Route. This activity makes apparent the different approaches individuals (or in this case, groups) take to achieve the same goal. The class should be divided into small groups to complete a simple task that has several solutions. Once the activity is over, they should think about and justify the reasons for the approach they took, including how they worked as a group. Such a task might be to move a tennis ball from one table to another, set up in the following way. Place several straws on the table with the ball and issue the instruction that they can use anything in the room, but must not touch the ball with their hands. Some may find ways to use the straws, others may use other tools, and some may just use their elbows to pick up the ball.

When coaching, it might be tempting for the children to offer each other 'solutions' to issues. As will be witnessed in the above activity, a particular approach may not necessarily be right for others and could instantly disempower them, in terms of their perceived ability to solve their own issues or by negating the will to find their own solution.

Instead of the temptation of offering a solution, the children may find themselves tempted to ask 'well, what on earth is stopping you from doing that?' when they hear the issue to be resolved. Again, we all perceive challenges in different ways, so ideally a coach should not entertain such a thought. In reality at this stage, though, it is enough just not to communicate any judgement in order to maintain the rapport and the trust. Despite all this, a non-judgemental version of that question can prove very useful. 'What is stopping you?' prompts thinking by presuming that there must have been an obstacle for the coachee to have not already achieved this end. This question will either reveal to them poor excuses that they can dismiss as soon as mention, or issues that can be quickly resolved by answering a further challenging question. A third possibility is that a limiting belief will be revealed (see Chapters 14 and 15). This can be worked through in a number of ways with questions that challenge the belief (see examples pages 77 and 78). Movement has begun.

- Cycle Challenge. This is a tool that Simon has found particularly useful in quickly reaching a resolution to an issue (usually a problem to be solved). Amazingly, it only uses two questions, one of which is 'what is stopping you'? The other is 'what could you do'? However, this cycle of questions should be delivered carefully, with a conversational tone, as such a quick approach applied tersely could evoke a negative reaction in the coachee. Using the other person's name can help soften any potential misreading. This tool is also useful for 'coaching on the hoof' when there is little time to sit down and work through a more comprehensive session. The example below uses a scenario familiar to teachers.

Table 25.1 Cycle challenge

Coach	Coachee
	I can't finish the story.
What's stopping you, Tom?	My pen is not working.
What could you do?	Borrow another one.
What's stopping you?	I don't know who to ask.
What could you do?	Start asking people on my table.
What's stopping you?	Nothing, miss.

Uncovering a way forward

One of the coach's main jobs is to help the coachee find ways of reaching their goal. This may involve simply encouraging them to come up with some ideas from which they will select the one that is best for them. Sometimes, coachees need to be encouraged to view the way forward from another perspective. They may have dwelt on the issue previously and become stuck in a mindset (a set mind). It is important here that the coach remains positive and does not try to think for the coachee; s/he should be thinking of questions or techniques that will help shift perception. Below are some examples from earlier in the book.

- Problem Solver Grid (page 49)
- The Merlin Game (page 51)
- Another View. What would their best friend suggest in a situation like this? What about one of their parents?
- Counting Blessings (page 100). What from their list of personal qualities could help them find a way forward on this issue?

Prior to trying any of the above, a good opener for generating possible ways forward is simply, 'what *could* you do'? (note the emphasis – there should be no analysis of what is possible at this stage). The coach could add the instruction 'let your mind run wild!' One group of managers Simon was working with recently did just that and produced all kinds of unconventional solutions for work issues that eventually yielded practical solutions.

Planning for action

When the coachee has selected a way to progress towards their goal, a classic coaching checking procedure is to ask 'on a scale of 1 to 10, how committed are you to this course of action?' Obviously, a ten every time would be best; however, lesser numbers may reveal a flaw in the planning. Examining that now would save time later, and a more motivated coachee could emerge from the process. So, if the answer to the above question is a seven, then a follow-up question similar to 'what is the other three?' should take the conversation back into the productive realm of looking at possibilities.

The acronym 'SMART' is normally associated with goals or targets. It is likely that you would have used this at some point in your school career. We like to use this approach towards the end of the coaching session as a way of clarifying – for both the coach and coachee – what is to be done, when, with whom, checked against a larger goal (if appropriate) and to ensure the success is recognisable. It forms a connection between the original goal and the action to achieve it, which in a way becomes goal-like itself. The template we have created below is mainly self-explanatory. However, we have linked the 'Relevant' part of the action plan to the assumption that this outcome will probably move the coachee towards a larger goal and, for 'Achievable', we have changed the emphasis to mean 'what will make it more achievable?' As we know that telling someone our plans

Table 25.2 SMART

	Components	Key Questions	Plan
Action:	Specific	What exactly will you do?	Main details:
	Measurable	How will you know when you have achieved this? What will make it a success?	Success criteria:
	Achievable	Who will help you? With whom will you share your action plan?	Advocate:
	Relevant	How will this help you achieve your larger / ultimate goal?	Rationale:
	Timing	By when will you do this?	Date (and time?):

makes us more likely to see them through (e.g. we do not want to appear as if we have 'failed', or that we have let someone down, or we might simply appreciate support), we thought that asking this question would make the plan more achievable. We recommend children use this plan to get used to the idea of visualising their course of action.

You will notice in the SMART plan (page 110) it was mentioned that in order to reach a larger goal, smaller goals may first need to be achieved. This is desirable in that the distant destination is made more achievable when punctuated by smaller successes to be celebrated along the way.

- Life Chunks. Notice the chunks we use in life. Getting ready to go out, or to go on a picnic – what steps do the children go through? When doing a jigsaw, do they just launch into it, or are there smaller steps they take to reach the ultimate goal of having a completed picture in front of them? What other examples can they think of that require them to go through smaller chunks first? You could ask them to draw this out, perhaps as a staircase, labelling each stair on their way to reaching an ultimate goal.
- Step into the Future. Capture the value of mentally rehearsing the outcome by visioning the future and then seeing how you got there. Ask the children to remind themselves of the goal and to see / hear / feel it in all its glory. How long in the future is that? Next, ask them to take a step back nearer to the present. What did they have to achieve to reach that point? Now come a little closer to the present. What was done to reach that point? There are a number of ways of running this activity, including using agreed timings into the future and literally stepping between the times.

Example coaching conversation (Part Two)

Below is a continuation of the conversation begun on page 106. Once again, this is only one example of how a coaching session might develop, as questions will vary with the responses, the content and the skills of the coach.

- Dissecting a Coaching Conversation (2). This is another opportunity for discussion about what the children notice about this conversation.

There are some interesting features that may be picked up in the exchange. Again, it can be seen that the coach has leeway to respond to what the coachee says in order to get enough information for the next useful question to be asked. Coaches should never ask information questions that satisfy their own curiosity – this is usually a sign that the coach is trying to solve the problem for the coachee. The main landmarks appear in this conversation, notably the 'what *could* you do?' and 'what *will* you do?' question types. At the stage of generating possible courses of action, the coach was constantly striving for more by asking 'what else?' (note, not 'is there anything else?' as this closed question could allow an easy exit for the coachee; the open question presupposes that there is at least one other possibility). When the coachee signals that there are no more ideas, s/he is instructed to give 'three more'. Again, presupposition plays a part and the coachee will usually find at least one more possibility. Sometimes, this is the one that is eventually chosen.

Table 25.3 Coaching conversation 2

Coach	Coachee
What's stopping that from happening?	I haven't made any friends at school since I started here and so I'm not usually involved with the laughter.
What would make it better?	To have some friends at school.
Who would you like to be friends with?	There is a group of three girls in my class who seem nice, but I haven't spoken to them yet.
What *could* you do?	Speak to them.
How might you go about doing that?	Well, I could go over and talk to them.
Good. What else?	I could ask if I could join in with their games at break.
Good. What else?	I've noticed they like running around games, so I could tell them about a game we used to play at my old school that they might not know.
Good. What else?	I can't think of anything else.
Just tell me three more	Well, they all play for the school football team, so I could go along to practice.
Good. What else?	Beth lives near me. I could ask her if she wants a lift to school.
Good. What else?	I really can't think of any more.
That's fine. You've done really well. You've come up with five ideas. Which of those appealed to you most?	Going to football practice. It doesn't feel as scary as the others and I think I might be quite good at football.
What *will* you do?	It's on a Monday night, so I'll check with my parents and then give it a go.
What will you do to make friends while you are there?	It will be easier to talk, so I'll just make sure I find the opportunity.
Great, so tell me what your plan is as you write it down on your SMART sheet.	• I'm going to go to football practice on Monday night and will talk to the girls and, hopefully, get on well with them (specific and measurable with timing). • I'll tell my parents what I'm doing to make sure I don't get cold feet (achievable) • If we become friends, it will move me very close to my overall goal of feeling happy at school (relevant).

Another point that might be picked up is the use of SMART, which clarifies the commitment and closes the session.

To recap on this section, we see it as dividing into three key areas:

- Starting the wheels rolling by finding out what is blocking the coachee or has helped them so far.
- Generating possible routes that might simply mean asking a question, or that may require an imaginative technique to lift the coachee out of the rut in which their (negative?) musings may have left them languishing.
- Selecting the road to take and then committing to it with a SMART action plan.

Quick questions to help you to get there:

What is stopping you?

What has helped so far?

How *might / could* you do that?

What *will* you do?

Who could help you?

Who could you tell?

How will you know when you have achieved this?

How committed are you to this course of action (on a scale of 1 to 10)?

Figure 25.1 QQ how will you get there

CHAPTER

26

How did it go?

Coaching is a very personalised form of learning. New insights can occur at any point in the process and will be acknowledged then. However, building in time for reflection when a goal has been achieved will reinforce the learning and allow new details to emerge. Like coaching, thinking reflectively can help raise awareness of our attitudes, actions and their impact and, as we have pointed out so often in this book, that is an important element of emotional intelligence.

- Reflective Diary. To encourage the habit of reflection, you might suggest that the children keep diaries of their day-to-day lives or on a specific topic (e.g. the progress of a sport or hobby they have recently taken up). Re-reading their entries will help them appreciate how situations develop and how choices and actions affect outcomes. This will assist the development of strategic thinking for the future.

The key to any reflection is to look back clearly. At some time we imagine most people would have highlighted the negative, which skews perception and the learning they take away from it. Dividing the main question of 'how did it go?' into two should help provide that balance. Those two questions are 'what went well?' and 'what could have been better?'

- Maintaining Balance. Ask the children to divide a sheet of paper in two and write those two questions at the top of each column. They should now look back on the actions and outcomes of the coaching. The notes they make need to be honest, immodest and precise. When this is completed, pair up the children to ask each other about their reflections. They are looking to stimulate further insight, so prompts like 'tell me what happened here' and 'if you were to do this again, how would you do it differently next time?' will be useful.

How individuals deal with setbacks is an indicator of their resilience. With some straightforward reframing, however, the resilience disposition can become accessible to all. Tell the children to forget dwelling on judgements of supposed 'failure' (if that is what they do), and simply remember to ask themselves the question 'what did I learn?' and 'how can I use that?' With practice, they will soon adopt a more resourceful attitude. Conversely, when their actions have led to success, acknowledging that can be a motivator and reinforce resolve for further goals. They might choose to celebrate this in some way. A fun activity is to agree how they will reward themselves when they achieve their goal, as part of the coaching process. If they included someone in their action plan to help make their goal more achievable, then that person's praise will further add to the feelings of achievement.

Metacognition

This word – meaning thinking about the thinking process – describes an activity that can be carried out in a number of ways for the benefit of exploring our own thoughts and motives. Obviously, it can be extremely beneficial after actions have been taken. Just thinking about the thoughts may not be enough. Noting them down, having to articulate and order them, perhaps relating them to any subsequent actions and their impact, would be of more use. Using guidance questions (such as 'what did I do?', 'what brought me to that decision?' and 'what happened?') is one approach. Another is to use a visual representation, like a flowchart annotated with explanations next to key decisions and reflections running along the side of the process. A key question after such metacognitive enquiries is 'what, if anything, will I do differently next time?'

Transfer

Sometimes the children will hit on a way of moving towards a goal that seems novel, exciting and full of potential. It may be a technique, an approach to a situation, or perhaps a choice of words. If it works well, they should ask themselves 'where else might this be useful?' They might begin by thinking of areas in life where they feel stuck, then ask 'how might this work there?' and, again, allow their minds to explore the possibilities. It may not necessarily be right for those areas, but considering it as if it might be will allow the mind to search for possible ways of linking it and may arrive at other new possibilities.

The other side to all this is that the new approach might not have worked, leaving them surprised and perhaps a little disappointed. It would be crazy to abandon an idea that appeared to have so much potential, so the question to ask in this case should be 'where might this approach prove more successful?' and let their minds run wild once again.

Quick questions to reflect on how it went:

How did it go?

What worked well?

What could have been better?

What did you learn?

What will you do differently next time?

Figure 26.1 QQ how did it go

Figure 3.1 Spot the difference solution

Notes

Chapter 1: EI basic skills

1   Although strictly speaking coaching techniques acknowledge that 'the future starts now' and that our power to decide exists in the present moment, the questions we ask, the options we consider and the conclusions we reach would not be possible if we were not all, right now, the outcome of everything that has happened to us. Also, while coaching relies heavily on cognitive (conscious and rational) thinking skills, emotionally intelligent people also tend to give value to the 'fuzzier' elements of their insights; hunches, intuitions, gut feelings and so on, which are the outcomes of subconscious activity, consciously perceived. Acknowledging these elements allows us to play with possibilities and their positive outcomes instead of being tempted to dismiss viable options as impractical at an early stage in our explorations. We feel that to deny the qualities the subconscious offers and try to rely solely on conscious logical thought would severely limit a person's ability to become more aware of oneself and others. (For more insight into coaching and its principles, see Section 2).

2   If a child says 'I can't' or 'I don't know', prompt her by saying 'Well pretend you do and tell me when you know'. The 'pretend' bit makes it safe and the 'when' is a presupposition that the child will succeed. This notion is linked to the so-called 'triangle of failure', see page xx.

Chapter 3: Encouraging creativity

1   Many children, and adults too, hold on to the limiting idea that other people make them angry (or whatever); in other words that they are at the mercy of their own reactions, and by extension at the mercy of what other people say and do. One benefit of becoming more emotionally resourceful is that people learn to take more responsibility for their own behaviour – using the word to mean 'the ability to respond'. Once children feel that they have the capability to be angry or not, they have already made a vital transition to a more resourceful state.

2   Like becoming better at most things in life, developing EI requires application. People are organisms not machines and achieve outcomes by often complex and sometimes tortuous means. The techniques in our book are tools (to use a common metaphor) not formulas. And depending on all kinds of factors every child's progress is likely to be different. When was a learning curve ever curve shaped?

Chapter 4: Conscious and subconscious

1   This technique is in no way frivolous. Its effectiveness rests partly on the notion that 'perception is projection'; that our perceptions are filtered through a pre-existing 'map of reality' in each of our heads, most of it lying at a subconscious level. In other words the world reflects what we think the world is like.

Chapter 6: Developing resourcefulness

1   The writer and visionary, the late Arthur C. Clarke said that the progress of science has in the past been hindered by failures of imagination and nerve. Much of his work was devoted to envisioning a future where such failures had been overcome.

2   When Steve runs thinking / creative writing workshops in schools he'll quite often have a child come up to him and say 'But I can't do this'. His reply is invariably 'Well pretend you can and tell me when you've done it'. This little linguistic trick usually bypasses failures of imagination and nerve: 'pretend' makes it safe while the word 'when' is a *presupposition of success*, which communicates to the child (sometimes only subconsciously) that expectations are high and completing the task well is inevitable.

Chapter 7: Raising self-awareness

1   The five main elements of mind mapping® are –
- Different kinds or categories of information are placed in different parts of the visual field.
- The ideas are colour coded for easier visual access.
- Key words are used to 'anchor' related ideas.
- Pictures representing these ideas are added nearby.
- Creative links are made between otherwise disparate ideas.

Chapter 8: Take responsibility

1   Steve drafted a number of writer's rights in his book Countdown to Creative Writing. They are –
- The right to learn in your own way.
- The right to say 'I don't understand'.
- The right to make mistakes (realising that that mistakes can have great learning value).
- The right to change your mind.
- The right to accept advice if it helps you to learn, and to reject advice that isn't useful.
- The right to judge your own behaviour (when you are willing to take responsibility for the consequences of your actions).

Chapter 9: Building confidence and belief in yourself

1   When Steve makes author visits to schools he is increasingly (and disappointingly) asked if he's a) rich b) famous and c) won any awards. These perceived criteria of success strike him as being a sad reflection of our modern culture.

2   Whenever Steve is asked if he thinks he's a better writer than X, he paraphrases something George Bernard Shaw once said, that 'I am only a fellow traveller along the same road.

We might walk at different paces and cover different distances, but we're all going in the same direction'.

Chapter 11: Nurturing a positive outlook

1   Stay on your toes with this. When we ran this activity in one class a child immediately piped up with 'Well I'm not going to give Miss any homework for tonight, so I don't expect her to give me any'.

2   Having said that, the human imagination can effect powerful changes to a person's outlook, such that our acts of make-believe serve to *make beliefs*. As Henry Ford said 'Whether you think you can or think you can't, you're right'. See also the reference to self-fulfilling prophecies in Section 15 Overcoming Obstacles.

3   Though we can't resist quoting W.C. Fields who said 'Start every day with a smile – and get it over with!'

Chapter 12: How we shape ourselves

1   A key concept in Transactional Analysis is 'the Script', or life plan, the pattern for which is laid down in childhood. However at the core of TA are the convictions that people can change, and we have a right to be in the world and be accepted.

Chapter 16: The winged football and other metaphors

1   Fascinatingly the same teacher admitted a certain nervousness herself when it came to creative writing. 'I really don't like committing my thoughts to paper'. Steve pointed out, with no trace of malicious glee, that the word 'committed' was also commonly used when referring to crime or the burial of a body.

2   The word can be usefully thought of as re-cognition, 'bringing again into conscious awareness'. This is where realisations can occur and where cognitive work-of-change is carried out.

3   This word can be thought of as 'making real' in one's conscious life.

Chapter 20: Really listening

1   This is not about blaming individuals, but about finding out what happened and so discovering what everybody can learn from it.

Bibliography

(Note that the editions quoted are the ones we used in our research)

Bloom, B. *The Taxonomy of Educational Objectives*, London: Longman, 1956.

Bowkett, S. *If I Were a Spider*, Stafford: Network Educational Press (now London: Continuum), 2004.

Bowkett, S. *Emotional Intelligence*, PocketPal series, London: Continuum, 2007.

Bowkett, S. *Jumpstart! Creativity*, Abingdon, Oxon: Routledge, 2007.

Bowkett, S. *Countdown to Creative Writing / Countdown to Poetry Writing / Countdown to Non-Fiction Writing*, Abingdon, Oxon: Routledge 2008–2009.

Bowkett, S. *Developing Literacy and Creative Writing through Storymaking: Story Strands for 7–12 Year Olds*, Maidenhead, Berks: Open University Press / McGraw-Hill Education, 2010.

Briers, S. *Brilliant Cognitive Behavioural Therapy*, Harlow, Middlesex: Pearson Education, 2009.

Cameron-Bandler, L. & Lebeau, M. *The Emotional Hostage*, Moab, Utah: Real People Press, 1986.

Campbell, J. *The Power of Myth*, New York: Bantam, Doubleday, Dell, 1991.

Carnegie, D. *How to Stop Worrying and Start Living*, Tadworth, Surrey: World's Work, 1972.

Covey, S. *The 7 Habits of Highly Effective People*, London: Simon & Schuster, 1999.

Gallwey, W. T. *The Inner Game of Work*, New York: Texere, 2002.

Honoré, C. *In Praise of Slow*, London: Orion, 2005.

National Advisory Committee on Creative and Cultural Education, *All Our Futures: Creativity, Culture & Education*, Sudbury, Suffolk: DfEE Publications, 1999.

O'Connor, J. and Seymour, J. *Introducing Neuro-Linguistic Programming*, London: Mandala (HarperCollins), 1990.

Owen, N. *The Magic of Metaphor*, Bancyfelin, Carmarthen, Wales: Crown House, 2001.

Paley, V. G. *The Boy Who Would Be a Helicopter*, Cambridge, Mass.: Harvard University Press, 1991.

Propp, V. *Morphology of the Folktale*. Austin: University of Texas Press, 2001.

Rockett, M. and Percival, S. *Thinking for Learning*, Stafford: Network Educational Press, 2002.

Rogers, J. *Coaching Skills: a handbook*, Maidenhead: Open University Press, 2005

Rotter, J. B. *Social Learning and Clinical Psychology*. New York: Prentice-Hall, 1954

Stanley, S. & Bowkett, S. *But Why? Developing Philosophical Thinking in the Classroom*. Stafford: Network Educational Press, 2004.

Stock, G. *The Book of Questions*, New York: Workman Publishing Company, 1987.

Thomas, W. and Smith, A. *Coaching Solutions*, Stafford: Network Educational Press, 2004

Tolle, E. *The Power of Now*, London: Hodder & Stoughton, 2005.

Twenge, J. M., Zhang, L., and Im, C, 2004, *It's beyond my control: A cross-temporal meta-analysis of increasing externality in locus of control, 1960–2002*, Personality and Social Psychology Review, 8, pp 308–19

UNICEF, *Child poverty in perspective: An overview of child well-being in rich countries, Innocenti Report Card 7*, UNICEF Innocenti Research Centre, Florence, 2007

Van Slyke, E. *Listening to Conflict*, New York: Amacom, 2009

Wallas, L. *Stories for the Third Ear*, New York: Norton, 1985.

Whitmore, J. *Coaching for Performance*, London: Nicholas Brealey Publishing, 2002

Whitworth, L., Kimsey-House, H. and Sandahl, P. *Co-active Coaching* Palo-Alto: Davies-Black, 1998

Williams, P. *How Stories Heal* (audiobook), London: Human Givens Publishing, 2009.

Index